TOUGH LOVE

TOUGH LOVE

BILL MILLIKEN
with Char Meredith

Fleming H. Revell Company
Old Tappan, New Jersey

Library of Congress Catalog Card Number: 68-17092
Printed in the United States of America

Preface

THREE THINGS I feel need to be expressed to you before you read this book. I must start by making something quite clear. This isn't really my book, but the book of many. The book belongs to the young men and women of New York City's Lower East Side, for they have been the teachers and it is largely their thoughts that have been shared on the pages that follow. I have simply had the privilege of being the string that runs through the manuscript.

Secondly, I must confess that I came here eight years ago to help people, only to find that I was the one who needed the most help; to bring change, only to find myself being the one who has had to change and has been changed the most. I came to the Lower East Side with one set of eyes, only to find that my vision was partially distorted and that Christ has had to give me a new pair of eyes along with an ability to listen through a sharper set of ears. Many of the years have been spent erasing old ideas and clichés that I came to the city with, allowing Christ to teach me His truth and seeing the problems of society exposed from His point of view.

Finally, it has become evident to me that if the church is to regain its relevance in our time it must leave the comfortable place it has found itself in—hiding behind the skirts of the status quo—sitting safely on the shore of life fishing for guppies. We must break out once again and place ourselves on the frontier of existence where Christ has called the church to be down through the ages—to launch our lives out into the deep waters, where security does not exist, to fish for men. Christ knows where the fish are and He is our security. I believe George McLeod best expressed it many years ago when he said:

"I simply argue that the cross be raised again, at the center of the marketplace as well as on the steeple of the church. I am rediscovering the claim that Jesus was not crucified in a cathedral between two candles, but on a cross between two thieves, on the town garbage heap, on a crossroad so cosmopolitan that they had to write His title in Hebrew and in Latin and in Greek, or shall we say, in English, in Bantu, and in Africaans—at the kind of place where cynics talk smut, the thieves curse and soldiers gamble, because that is where He died, and that is what He died about, and that is where Christians should be and what Christians should be about."

My greatest hope is that by my peeling the onion of the city layer by layer, exposing its problems, fears, frustrations as well as its gold, potential and "soul"—you may see the city from a new point of view, and that this new insight may motivate action on your part. I hope, too, that you may be able to weep and pray over our cities as Christ once wept over Jerusalem; that some of the myths we have come to believe concerning our city dwellers may be erased, and that you may learn from the inside out to walk in their shoes and in so doing gain hope and positive direction in a time when so many eyes are turned in despair on the ghettos of our nation.

There are *many* people to thank for their help in making this book possible. There are, of course, Char Meredith and my wife, Jean, as well as Mr. Fred Bauer of *Guideposts* magazine and Mr. Bill Starr, the Executive Director of Young Life Campaign. I also want to thank the many friends on our Young Life staff who have helped direct my life over the years, and I especially want to express my gratitude to the young men and women of the Lower East Side, those mentioned and the many who will remain anonymous, who are the real authors of this book!

Contents

Introduction

THIS AMAZING twentieth-century chronicle is as relevant and up-to-date as tomorrow morning's *New York Times,* yet it is rooted in the timeless principles of the New Testament. It is the story of a great city, a young man, and God.

Tough Love describes the God who has revealed Himself in Jesus Christ, and it sums up the story of a child—conceived by an unmarried Judaean village girl—who grew up to be a carpenter; who loved people and helped them, and who was finally executed publicly because He insisted that He was the Son of God.

Tough Love is also the story of a young man from an affluent home in a Pittsburgh suburb, who met the Carpenter and found a new life and a new direction.

It tells about the God who led Bill Milliken to a unique ministry on New York City's Lower East Side. It shows how God revealed Himself further to Bill through the people of the inner city.

This is also the story of many who met the Carpenter through Bill: people whose lives were changed, and who became involved in a quiet revolution.

It is a book that I long for everyone to read. Bill and his friends are a challenge to Christians who need to discover the relevance of Christ in new ways; to social workers who need to find more potent methods of uncovering and meeting people's needs; to psychologists who need new tools to motivate individuals and help them become whole; and to anyone who loves the inner city and would like to discover its true heart and its true potential.

I am grateful for the experience of knowing Bill Milliken, and of seeing the God of the city through his eyes. I am glad that the same experience is now possible for all who will read this book.

Bruce Larson

New York City
June 10, 1968

1
Born to Move

It took me a long time to discover that love could be tough.

In fact, it took me a long time just to discover what love really was. I suppose that sounds crazy, because Bill Milliken's one guy who sure didn't come from a deprived situation. By most people's standards, I had it made. I was White Anglo-Saxon Protestant. I grew up in the middle class suburb of Wilkinsburg, Pennsylvania. My father owned a good business he'd have been glad to welcome any of us three kids into. I had two older brothers I looked up to, and, being the youngest in the family, I was usually allowed to get away with murder. I used my home as a roof and a meal ticket, and gave my parents little chance to know me. Maybe that was because in those days I didn't know myself.

My parents didn't make me go to church, so I seldom bothered. People who went to church didn't look or act much different to me from people who stayed away. They looked nice and dressed up on Sunday, but I saw what they did the rest of the week. And as for Christ and all that stuff about the gospel of love, what little I listened to I didn't really understand. It sounded weak and sentimental. I didn't see much sense in following a man always portrayed in a skirt. I didn't know then that it took a real Man to love as Christ had done, and that it took guts to follow Christ—in the first century, and in the twentieth.

I found out loving is tough—it costs; and the love itself has to be tough, too, tough enough to hurt if the hurt can heal. When I was a teen-ager I thought I knew all about being tough (and all about hurting, too). Being the youngest in both the family and the gang I hung out with, I was continually running to catch up, and it was a constant effort for me to maintain status. I learned how to hang out, how to make it with the older guys, how to be the brunt of occasional ridicule too. Being the youngest made me feel for any person who was supposed to lose, the one who got pushed around or ganged up on. Rejection always caused me to hurt inside, but I felt bad only because it made me hurt too. I didn't know enough to do anything about their hurt. People around me got the impression I was always happy, for I had my dad's warm, friendly personality, but there were times when I hated life.

One night during high school, when my older brother Bob told me he wanted to take me to a Young Life club over in another part of town, I shrugged my shoulders and said, "Why not?" Something had happened to Bob, and occasionally I wondered what it was. He had decided he wanted to be a minister, and was attending seminary. I thought maybe Young Life club could give me a clue to what had caused the change. The night I went for the first time, club was being led by a friend of Bob's named Jerry Kirk. His warm smile got through to me right away. We became better friends as he began to hang out at the high school and local pool hall. After a few months he zeroed in on me with an offer: "Bill, you get four of your friends to go along with you, and I'll see that all five of you guys get out to Colorado this summer to a ranch. Would you like that?"

No second invitation was necessary! Two months later, I was on my way to an experience that changed my life. Those Colorado ranches are an integral part of Young Life's program and, now that I'm a Young Life leader myself, I never cease being grateful for their existence. I didn't see too much of Jerry after we got to the ranch; he counseled with the guys from the other side of town, and a guy named Mal got our Wilkinsburg gang. There was something about both those guys that reached out and grabbed me. In fact, everything about the place was grabbing me—the mountains, the tremendous kids from high schools all over the United States, the excitement that continued all day and into the night, the lovely girls, and free pool tables. But the down-to-earth talks about important things in life were what really struck home. I discovered how many misconceptions I'd had about God, and found myself taking a surprising interest in Him. The first thing I knew, I'd been duped into getting hooked up with Him! I was really mixed up.

Then Mal explained to me how much Christ loved me, and how Christ was one and the same with God. I had a lot of new ideas to think about. I felt I was surrounded with love. When those guys talked about Christ, He was not some far-off impossible character out of a Sunday-school lesson, or a musty old critic out to kill a good time; He was a real flesh-and-blood Friend.

By the end of the week I walked off alone into the vast Rocky Mountain night and sort of threw out a divine dare: "Christ, if You're real, I wish You'd do something in my life, because I sure need it!"

The leaders strongly urged that I be given a place on the work crew so I could stay on at Frontier Ranch for several more weeks. They feared I wasn't strong enough in my newfound faith to go home and face the crowd. This was the most thrilling news of my life. At the time, I had little idea of how much I needed more time to think and to learn. It's almost foolish to try to explain the new quality of life that pulled us together on work crew that summer, whether we were washing dishes, cleaning johns, building the swimming pool, or off at the top of the world snow-sliding. Life had never been so vivid; I had never felt so real. It was my first experience of what genuine Christian fellowship is all about. As the time for returning home approached, I began feeling almost measurable degrees of sadness. I had tasted something so great. I had found something so real. And I was scared it was all going to stay there in the mountains while I rode off across the flat midwest plains to Pittsburgh. I wanted to stay at Frontier Ranch forever.

Back in high school that fall I messed up time and time again, but my desire to be Christ's remained strong. Right away that fall, I started attending a Young Life club and we averaged eighty kids at our meetings all that year. My buddies ribbed me about getting elected president of that first Wilkinsburg club, but now and then some of them would turn up at club themselves.

One of the guys I really wanted to get through to was Lee Maxwell. We used to hang out together at Nobbie's Pool Hall, and I was elated when I talked him into going to Colorado with me that summer. The afternoon we were to leave, Lee got so bombed I had to carry him onto the train. But once we got to Frontier Ranch the same thing happened to him that had happened to me the year before. Lee began to see that there was something better in life than drinking, and hot-rodding, and making out in the back seat of a car. Such a change took place in him that summer that for the next five years we were still getting guys to come to Young Life on the basis of the change Christ had made in the life of that one high-school friend!

As for me, I got off to a bad start on the trip out, even before we reached the ranch. An ex-marine rode out on the train with us—a rough guy, but I thought he was square. I didn't like his strictness about doing every little thing right. When we were assigned to our duties at the ranch, he turned out to be my work crew boss!

The showdown came one morning when we were shoveling dirt off the end of a truck to fill up holes in the road. I was only throwing a shovelful every so often, and the boss had had it up to his chin. "Milliken, you're lazy!"

Wham! My next shovelful of dirt just accidentally happened to catch him full in the face! He lunged toward me and I flung the shovel at him. He ordered me back to the cabin and told me I would be shipped home.

Back in the cabin I was mad, embarrassed, and furious at myself for letting my temper go—usually I was able to cover my bad temper with a nice, phony front. The boss came down to talk to me, and it was all I could do to stand there and listen while he was talking. But he must have gotten through to me, because I wound up doing what he told me to: filling a wheelbarrow full of trash from the girls' washroom and pushing it the two miles to the garbage pit.

Needless to say, a howling audience watched me. I was as mad as could be inside. What was really bugging me was the fact that for the first time in my life an adult had let me have it straight;

I was used to this from kids, but not from grown-ups. All during that humiliating trip to the dump and back, I thought about going straight to the head of the whole Young Life organization to complain. I wanted to get up before a whole council of the leaders and tell them all how phony they were. I'd been hurt, and he'd stood up to me, and I wanted everybody to pay.

The staff had a big meeting over this incident and decided that instead of sending me home, they would stick it out with me. Through the community of people who wanted me to make it, through the consistency of that boss, and his own good humor, I eventually was able to apologize to him. When I did my work well, he was right there to tell me. When I didn't, he made me toe the line. I was always inconsistent, but he was not. He was the first person to demonstrate tough love to me, and I began to respect him for it.

The summer of 1959 I put in ten weeks at the Young Life ranch as assistant work crew boss. The hard schedule and constant close associations with kids and leaders opened up a lot of chances for me to look at myself. What I saw bugged me a lot. I fought to be myself, to find out who Bill Milliken was. It was particularly important at this point, because I had just graduated from high school and had to decide in what direction I was going.

I had goofed around a lot all through school, and my grades had been really bad in the beginning of my senior year. But as the result of one of my escapades I was put on detention for some time. Those two hours after school each day proved to me that if I sat down and studied I could do the work I was supposed to. The discipline, tough to accept, taught me how much more I could do when I had a firm structure to help me. That detention was the turning point in my grades; I went on to make the honor roll, pass my college boards, and get accepted at the University of Pittsburgh. Now I was hung up between my own desire to live freely and the rest of the world's insistence on shoving me into the old college mold.

The rest of the world won, and I started at the U. that fall. Six weeks into the first semester the conflicting pressures got too much for me, and I blew. I took off for Florida and struggled like crazy to find out who I was.

What was I doing there? Where was I going? Who the hell was Bill Milliken, anyway? I walked along Florida's sandy roads, kicking up the gravel as though somewhere, lurking under some stone, might be the answers to the questions that were tearing me apart.

My parents hardly knew me. The girls in my life were sick and tired of red roses one week and rumors of a new love the next. My teachers saw me floundering. My buddies stood by to watch. It was my battle; we all knew that in the final analysis it was up to me to win it, or to lose myself.

I had been born to move, to adventure. Even after those summers at the ranch I had little desire to get involved in anything that would cost me very much. But something inside me was crying to be born. That's what landed me on that sandy little wilderness road in Florida. The trip has always remained a mystery to my family and friends, but it was necessary for me. I only stayed away three weeks, but that was enough. The pressure was released, and that year was the best one I had ever had in any school. I made a B average and did well on the wrestling team. At the same time I was able to face the fact that I still had a lot of problems.

In the spring of that freshman year I bumped into Harv Oostdyk, a Young Life leader I'd met at the ranch the summer before. Some of the best things that had happened there had come through my friendship with Harv and with Vinnie Pasquale, a former narcotics addict from Newark, New Jersey. Harv had this vision of starting Young Life in New York City, and he got us excited about someday working with him among street kids. I was fascinated with the stories Harv and Vinnie told.

When Harv and I met again at a Young Life camp in New York State, he asked if I was still interested in working in the city, and I told him, "Sure!" It was that simple. A couple of months later I got a postcard telling me to come. I packed a few things and on June 17, 1960, I started East.

When I reached Harv's house in New Jersey nobody was home,

so I hunted up Vinnie at the Newark YMCA where he worked part-time. That night the two of us went to Oostdyk's. We talked so late that we finally fell asleep on Harv and Emmy's floor!

The next morning we grabbed a basketball and started across the George Washington Bridge to look for some kids who wanted to shoot baskets. We had no idea what would happen.

2

Sharp Knives and a Dull Conscience

TAP AND Bobo Nixon were typical of the guys I was about to meet on New York's Lower East Side. In the huge Smith Project where they lived, the older guys belonged to the Centurions, of which the Young Pagans were the junior gang. About a mile north was the turf of the Sportsmen, whose superiority was undisputed on the whole Lower East Side.

By a strange fluke of luck the Young Pagans got tied in with the Sportsmen for a while. Bobo Nixon developed an intense hatred for a guy named Eddie, a Young Pagan who was separated from the gang. They became arch-enemies because of what happened one night when the Young Pagans were supposed to fight the Italian Warriors. All the Young Pagans—about fifty—showed up. Five of the O-heads (older guys) of the Sportsmen came down to the corner of Henry and Catherine Streets for a war council and two members of the opposing gangs were already tearing into each other when somebody yelled that the cops were coming.

Any time someone says, "The Man!" everybody makes it—and this night they made it, all of them. Most of the Young Pagans thought the war was over and went back to the project, but Eddie didn't have anything special to do that particular night so he just walked around. The O-heads of the Sportsmen were still hanging out in the project, so he took up with them. Fifteen minutes later, without any warning, a large gang of the Italians converged on the six. They got some of them, and the rest escaped.

Later, when they sat down to figure out what had happened,

the O-heads decided the Young Pagans had punked out on them, so they turned against them. However, since Eddie was the only one who didn't punk out, they kept him. That meant Eddie was in the tough position of fighting *with* the Sportsmen *against* the very guys he lived with in the project.

This gave him a reputation, and Bobo, as president of the Young Pagans, was personally out to get him. His feelings were so strong, in fact, that he was determined to kill Ed. They attended the same junior high school, but for some reason they never fought at school.

At least once a month some guy would come up to Eddie and say, "Hey, Ed!"

"Yeah, Babe. What's happening?"

"I hear you been talking about my mother."

"No, man. I haven't been talking about your mother."

"Yeah, man, this is what the fellows been saying to me."

"No, Babe. Not me."

"Well, Ed, we gotta fight, 'cause I believe the fellows."

So Eddie would have to fight him. This usually alternated between the same two guys, but it was never Bobo. Eddie used to be called Robin Hood or Sherlock Holmes because he used to wear a cape and an outlaw hat, and smoke a pipe. This was all part of the image he developed to gain self-confidence. When they went to a fight he would saunter, never run, even if his gang was outnumbered, even if all the others ran. He was really scared, really shook, but he never let the guys know how he felt inside. They all said Ed had a lot of "heart." Ed, the guy they could count on. Ed, the dependable leader.

Often Bobo would try to catch Ed going to the store, or just moving about the neighborhood. He would stay up late at night waiting for him, but somehow Bobo was always upstairs, or at a dance, when Eddie came home. Bobo had such a strong feeling inside him about this guy. He had never killed anybody yet—oh, sure, he had felt like it at times, and he had done some shooting in a crowd, but he didn't think he'd ever actually killed somebody—and there was no question in his mind about the fact that he was out to do Eddie in. He hated Eddie, and he wanted everyone to hate him. Eddie knew this, and he returned the compliment.

St. Christopher's Episcopal Church on Henry Street was one of the neighborhood's community centers. Many teen-agers gathered there to play Ping-Pong, basketball, or pool, or to dance and talk. Father Dwyer, and Father Myers before him, acted on their conviction that "to follow the way of love means to leave one's self open to the hostility of the unloved." Their story is one of a persistent attempt by a small group of Christians to overcome the hate and fear among the people of its parish. In Bobo and Eddie's battle, St. Chris' served successfully as a truce ground.

Almost as quickly as their hostility had flared, an enduring friendship was born between them.

Both were hired by the church that summer—Bobo took on custodial duties, and Ed was working with ten- and eleven-year-olds in a vacation recreational program. For some reason, everything was very cool in the neighborhood that summer, and in the course of duty the two boys got acquainted on an entirely different basis. They both became part of Tap's singing group, and this gave them further constructive outlets together.

In the fall, when fighting broke out again, Eddie stayed with the guys in the Smith Project. "I put the Sportsmen down, man! I want to be with you." The older Centurions were fading out of the gang picture, which allowed the Young Pagans to emerge as the older guys in the new Centurions, and to become the dominant gang for several years on the Lower East Side.

In those days of the late '50's and early '60's, the gang era faded to a close in New York City. But before it was completely played out, Eddie was seriously hurt in a war that broke out in front of St. Christopher's. After two war counselors got in an argument, a fight started without any warning. The Centurions were unarmed, not having expected to need their weapons, but the Sportsmen had stashed zip guns and chains in the garbage can. When the Centurions heard the yelling starting, they ran out of the church into the street.

Eddie had just made a zip gun, and he positioned himself on the stairs. He was ready to shoot when a priest came out and grabbed his hand. Almost at the same time, a guy with a knife darted up behind Ed and stabbed him. The blade bit deeply into Ed's hip and his leg buckled under him. Bobo was there when Eddie fell. He watched the blood staining his pants, and he hurt inside along with his best friend. Later, when he went to the hospital, he found Eddie boiling mad. "Don't you kill him, Bobo! He's all mine!"

After Ed was well enough to get out he and Bo started stalking the guy who had cut him. "We went all the way into the Sportsmen's territory," Bobo recalls. "Carried any kind of weapon we happened to have—out in the open. We didn't care about the Sportsmen; we didn't care about the cops; we didn't care about anything except doing that guy in."

Eventually they found out the knifer was in jail. Eddie was still seeking revenge when the guy got out six months later. They set up a fight, and Eddie won. This must have satisfied him, because after that they cooled it. The gang era was on its way out now, anyway. After the restless summer of '59, fighting took the form of single-handed combat, or small groups, rather than full-fledged wars. When there was a disagreement, the guys would usually set up a fair match, one guy against another, and nobody would jump in. It began to be accepted that two guys could settle their own grievances by fighting until one gave up.

The only way they knew to satisfy their hunger for excitement was to fight. "It didn't bother us in the least to smash a guy," Bobo explains. "I never thought about what I was doing. My conscience was just dull."

One of the things that helped me at first was my complete ignorance. I just didn't know how much I didn't know! If I had, I might never have had the guts to stick it out. When I heard a few guys singing in the park one day I went over and listened to them for the longest time. They kept staring at me, but went right on singing until I finally struck up a conversation by complimenting them enthusiastically on their group's sound. One of the fellows stayed around to talk after the others left, and I told him about Colorado.

That's the way we got the first ranch trip from New York started—we picked up one guy here, another there, from all different neighborhoods. I didn't know any of them, really, when the old bus rolled through Holland Tunnel to begin the two thousand mile run to Frontier Ranch.

It was a swinging trip. Some of those guys have fantastic wit. They had us in tears from laughing so hard, and they kept going for hours. But there was shock, too. I'd gone to Colorado three times with suburban kids, and once in a while somebody maybe would steal some little thing on the way. But *this* trip was an entirely different experience. I just took for granted that the guys were paying for their meals along the way. Later, at the end of the trip, I discovered most of them still had the five dollars' food allowance they'd been given when they left New York. Plus a little more they picked up gambling. Plus the fact that they'd eaten well all the way across the country!

I'd gotten nowhere trying to sell the Colorado trip to Bobo Nixon—he wouldn't give me the time of day—but I'd gotten Tap and Eddie to go along. I had no idea how much they hated whites when I asked them to go. When they said yes, I learned later, they'd just naturally figured they were headed for a predominantly black camp. When they got there and looked around, they saw only two black faces other than theirs, out of nearly two hundred kids!

That was their first shock, and others followed. In their minds the biggest reason for going to Colorado was to party; they'd heard enough to know they'd meet kids from all over the country, and go horseback riding and mountain climbing. That stuff had sounded pretty great. They hadn't bargained on getting really involved in the religious stuff. They had been to Young Life club twice in the city, and heard the talk about a personal relationship with Jesus Christ. Both times they had walked out in the middle. Like many guys and girls we meet on the streets, they had been dragged to church when they were little kids. As they got older, the church became a place to hang out, a recreation center where someone cared enough about kids to help them have a good time. But Jesus was Someone who stayed in the sanctuary while they took care of themselves.

The change from the brick and concrete of the city to the log cabins and mountain paths of the ranch is always a shock. Mountains and horses and pitch-black nights just aren't common to city kids. The friendliness and understanding of the people at Frontier Ranch also evoked unfamiliar feelings in Tap and Eddie. In fact, they first misread it as phony, because they had never been in a situation where people were so friendly. "I thought they were just doing all this because we were black," Eddie told me, "and they were just trying to be nice to us." Then he noticed everyone else was being treated the same way, too.

At first the guys tried to skip out of the "Round-up" meetings at night, but I happened to be right there when they started to cut out. The entertainment was funny, the singing was all right; but when leader Bob Mitchell started talking about this personal relationship with Christ, they began to get irritated.

One night in particular, Eddie wanted to leave the ranch so badly that nothing I could have said would have changed his mind; to this day neither of us knows what prompted him to go to Round-up, but he did. It turned out to be what he considers the most important night of his life. He began to think about things he had never considered before. Mitch was talking about the cross and how painful it was for Christ to be crucified. But what bit most deeply into Eddie's mind was the fact that the most painful thing was not the physical suffering of Christ, but the idea of those black, hellish hours of being forsaken by God. The force of the knowledge that Jesus Christ went through all of that for Ed Gist, that He would have done the same thing even if Ed Gist had been the only human being on earth, began to eat on his mind.

All during high school during the gang fights, Ed had looked for acceptance. In his family he had looked for love, but there never seemed to be enough to go around, and the only thing he felt for his father was animosity. Now here was Bob Mitchell telling him about Christ's suffering intensely just because He loved Ed Gist enough to bring him back into a relationship where God could make life good.

The next day Ed looked me up and we sat down and talked. Finally he said, "If God loves me this much, then I might as well give Him a chance to see what He can do in my life. I've been pretty messed up. I don't have any purpose. I don't know where I'm headed. All I really know is that I hate people. I hate my father more than anyone. I hate myself. If You can do anything with this life, Jesus Christ, well, then go ahead and do it!"

It sounded so much like my own "divine dare" of three years before! Tap accepted Christ too that week, and together the two of them made a scheme to convert all of their friends when they got back to New York—guys they had fought with in gang wars a few years earlier.

What happened was exactly the opposite. Back home the old friends sneered and said, "Yeah, we know you. You'll soon be back in the old groove again." They did not accept the new life Eddie was raving about, and the rejection was too much for him to take. Besides, he had expected a big emotional thing that would get him together personally. He expected everything to be better. When he got home he found out things had gotten even worse. Eddie told me later, "I saw something different in your life, and you said the difference was Christ. So I had to conclude that Christ must be real for some people and unreal for others. I had accepted Him into my life the way you had, but nothing had happened to make me any different."

Ed was always a rebel about everything. He quit school in the tenth grade because of gang fighting, and when he tried to go back he failed every subject. He failed in his Christian commitment just as miserably, and turned other kids against us too. "That's a white man's religion," he claimed. "I don't believe in it!"

Things went from bad to worse. Ed and his father had the worst fight of their lives that year. His dad would get high and do all sorts of weird things. One day the whole family attended a wedding, and Ed came in just as the reception ended to discover that his father had made trouble and his mother, to escape embarrassment, had locked herself in the bathroom and wouldn't come out. After Eddie succeeded in coaxing her out, his father wanted to take her to the bar with him.

"She's going home with me, Dad," Eddie said as they reached the bottom of the stairs on their way out.

Father didn't like son's tone any more than son liked father's attitude, so a fight began. Finally a brother-in-law jumped the older man and knocked him down. When he got back on his feet, he pulled out a long dagger and started chasing Eddie around a parked car. Suddenly Eddie whipped the aerial off a car and slapped his father across the face with it. As they ran, the blade kept flashing within inches of Eddie's tough young body, but the aerial was long enough to rip back and forth through flesh every time Ed turned around to defend himself. The blood was streaming down his father's face, and no one knows who would have gotten killed if the cops hadn't come. Ed's friends grabbed him and took him away before he got arrested.

He felt terrible about having had to fight his father, and this proved a very slight but significant turning point in his attitude toward other people. But during that year, Ed decided, "Well, enough for Christ. If He can't do anything to make my life different, then the hell with it!"

3

Getting Real

YOU COULDN'T have started a ministry with two worse, or weaker, people than Vinnie and I. No church board would have passed us as their youth workers. I certainly wasn't mature or stable, and the only job Vinnie had ever done was to push drugs! Yet God saw to it that we were where He wanted us. Many times He takes the least and works with them, and we definitely were in that category! Vinnie was still fighting his own problems. I was very lonely, and knew so little about involvement on a personal level. The two of us didn't even get along very well after our short association together.

I fought all the time against being a leader. I just didn't feel like one. I had never understood how I had come to be elected president of my class during my first year in high school. . . . I was really out of class with the other kids and had felt terribly embarrassed about it, particularly the day the candidates were introduced and I stood up in levis and a shirt with the collar up! I was so afraid of failing.

In the ghetto I found that sense of failure building up in me through rejection. I'd walk up to a guy on a park bench, and the guy would move away to avoid me. If I'd stick out my hand to shake hands, the guy would look away, pretending he didn't see. If I tried to join a group for basketball, all the other fellows would be chosen instead of me. For the first time in my life, I was running up against prejudice against *me*, and it hurt. The silent rejection was worse than overt action, for at least if somebody yelled at me or gave me a hard time there was interaction, dialogue—something could happen. This way, all my great ideas went down the drain and I felt so insecure.

When the rejections piled up to a certain point, I had to escape.

I remember one particular day going into a Broadway movie theatre to see *A Thousand Spartans*. I slouched down in the seat, my shoulders literally aching with defeat. The exciting action on the screen became a catharsis which built my ego way back up. I identified with those few Spartans who stood firm against the thousands and thousands of the enemy, and I felt strong. I was a Spartan, and the city was my enemy; the struggle was impossible, but we would hold. It was great—so long as I remained in the theatre. Once out in the street again, I sagged inside. The people were still there. The sickness was still there. And Bill Milliken was still there, just as insecure and afraid as he had been when he walked into the theatre.

I wandered over to Bryant Park, behind the New York Public Library, and dropped down on one of the stone benches. "God, just let me be me," I cried out in my heart. "Just Bill, even if it's a defeated Bill. Who am I? Where do I fit into the city?" It was so confusing, and the one thing I was struggling for was simply to be me, as God intended me to be—to accept myself as I was, and not be over-embarrassed about what I was not.

But first, I had to find out who I was.

That first fall on the Lower East Side, Vinnie and I took a little $32-a-month cold water flat. The building, like many in the neighborhood, was an old one which had been converted for multiple-family use, and it was definitely nothing like home! The bathtub was smack in the middle of the kitchen, and the toilet back in a corner. Vinnie and I pitched in to get the place cleaned and painted, and we managed to cram two beds and a dresser into the tiny space.

All this was a totally new experience for me. When I was a teen-ager I had gone wild with money, for there had always been plenty around whenever I needed anything. Now I was at the other extreme, for the money I had had in the bank when I left home was soon exhausted, and I began to see that poverty was a new kind of freedom. If there was money, we spent it; if there wasn't, we got along all right without it. Since we couldn't depend on money, I learned firsthand that money was not a real security.

As I got involved in the culture of the Lower East Side, I soon learned how to hustle. Often, if I was broke and hungry, I would turn up at a kid's house just in time for dinner. I was too proud to write home for help, but Dad and Mother would always give me money for birthdays and Christmas, and from time to time they would slip a few dollars into their letters. During that first full year of city living, I was down to fifty cents on seven different occasions, sometimes for as long as three or four days at a stretch. And I learned not to be afraid.

During that winter of 1960-61 I decided to go back to Pittsburgh for one trimester at the University. The apartment was given up, and Vinnie moved in with Father William Dwyer, priest-in-charge at St. Christopher's Episcopal Church on Henry Street. Father Dwyer wanted us down on the Lower East Side because he had become already familiar with the work of Young Life during his ministry at a suburban parish, and he had liked what he had seen. He was willing to do everything in his power to get us started in the inner city. When I returned to New York in April 1961, I found that Harv and Vinnie had started a little club to hold together the kids who had been to Colorado, plus a few others as well.

Other changes were taking place, too. During the summer Vinnie decided, at the age of 26, to go back to school, which he had quit at eighth grade. Vinnie's leaving left me without an apartment-mate, but I soon joined forces with Dean Borgman, an ex-paratrooper, from Bridgeport, Connecticut, who had a background much like mine. Dean had hung around with a bunch of suburban kids in trouble with the law both before and after his tour of duty. Now he'd gotten tired of having people ask him what he intended doing with his life—he couldn't say he just planned to hang around with kids!—so he had come to New York to work toward a doctorate on the G.I. Bill, with no definite direction in mind. He wound up in education and began teaching on the high-school level while doing graduate work at Columbia.

Dean and I took an apartment at 215 Madison Street (no resemblance to New York's Madison *Avenue!*). His younger brother, Dave, and a college buddy of mine moved in with us that summer to help. The four of us walked the streets, hour after hour after hour, and when we got tired of walking we sat on the benches in the park with the guys, or hung out at the basketball courts. Some people in the neighborhood thought we must be a new kind of cop; others decided we were social workers. One confessed recently, "I thought you were just plain stupid. My feelings toward you guys were all negative. I thought you were in a place where you didn't belong!"

We didn't belong, *yet*, but we were trying. Sometimes when we'd come home late at night to the suffocating heat of the tenement, we'd feel as if we weren't accomplishing anything at all, that we'd never be able to "get through" to real relationships, that we'd always be outsiders. Then Dave got acquainted with Clark Jones, a youth from the Smith Project.

Clark in a way was an outsider, too, for he didn't conform at all to the gang structure. He simply didn't care to drink or smoke pot; "I didn't feel I had to prove anything," is how he puts it. He and his friends enjoyed running through the hallways of the project playing tag, or going through all the wrestling holds they had watched on television. These "kiddie games" brought him ridicule from gang members and their girls, but even the toughest of them respected Clark because he could take care of himself and everyone knew it: "Nobody messes with Clark Jones 'cause he's good with his hands and he hits hard!"

Clark and his brother enjoyed hiking, barbecuing hot dogs, and horseback riding in Central Park—even going to a museum once in a while. Basketball was his favorite sport; in fact, he and some friends had just chosen sides and were taking foul shots in the big park near the project when Dave Borgman just walked up and began pulling down the rebounds and shooting baskets right along with them. After a couple of games he pulled Clark over to the side and asked, "Hey, Clark, how'd you like to take a trip to Colorado?"

Clark didn't have any idea where Colorado was, or who this

white stranger was, for that matter, but he did know he liked going on trips. He had gone camping and mountain climbing with his Boy Scout troop from the Catholic church to which his family belonged, and he liked going over to St. Christopher's to get in on some basketball or handball or occasional trips—he even went as far away as the YMCA on 23rd Street to get in on recreational activities there. Unlike most boys in his neighborhood, Clark had had a good teen-age life, and he was also different from most guys we approach in that he wanted to talk the Colorado idea over with his parents and get their opinion. After they gave their consent, Clark hunted Dave down again. "Hey, Borgman, is that trip to Colorado still open?"

"Sure. Do you want to go?"

"Yeah! Great! When do we leave? Right now?"

"Take it easy! In about a week."

"A week? That's forever! Let's go now if we're going to go!"

The trip to Colorado was the beginning of a real friendship between Dave and Clark. Dave owned a motorcycle which the two boys used to ride all over the place that summer—up into Connecticut, to the Borgman home, where a lot of Dave's friends had bikes too. It was beautiful, on a sunlit summer day, to look over a shoulder and see ten bikes all taking a curve together. When the time finally came for Dave to head back to college, Clark was heartbroken. Dave was the best friend he had ever had, and the means of his breaking out of the "walls of the inner city."

Dean and I were still there, of course, but for Clark it just wasn't the same. When I invited him up to the apartment for Bible study, he acted as though he wanted to tell me to go back where I'd come from. He put up with us only because he loved Dave and he loved Colorado. Dean and I could understand how difficult it was for Clark to switch his loyalty and affection from Dave to us, and we knew that he was definitely doing us a favor whenever he did cooperate.

As it turned out, Dean and I were alone at 215 Madison for only a short time. Frankie Santana, who had introduced me to the Young Dragons in his neighborhood, needed a place to stay, and so did his pal Ricky Rosario. Both of them had been on the trip to Colorado that summer, but as it turned out Frankie hadn't become a Christian because he was having too much fun fooling around with narcotics. Ricky, however, had gotten so interested in the Bible that he read all the way through it by himself, and then went through the New Testament two more times! Ricky was the strong man of the gang, the Gibraltar who could stand on the corner with the others while they were high, and never touch dope himself.

They asked us if they could move into the apartment. I fought it—not verbally, but inside myself. I knew their need; I felt compassion; I really wanted to help. But I also knew that if Frankie and Ricky moved into the apartment I would have no place to hide. They would see me as I really was. It would mean being on the job twenty-four hours a day.

We let them move in, and I soon found out how right my apprehensions had been. Dean and I had no place to escape to anymore. We couldn't leave the problems in the street and go home to rest; we went home to more problems. We went through failure after failure with both Ricky and Frankie, getting them started back in school, trying to keep them in school. Each failure hit us personally.

The day finally came when I heard through the grapevine that Ricky was high. I nearly dropped the transmission on my blue Comet getting over to him in the park. My hurt must have shown in my face. In defensiveness and guilt Ricky lashed out at me: "You're not my father, and I can do anything I want! Leave me alone!" I went home, hurting bad inside.

Much later, I learned from Ricky that he had been depressed because, although he had accepted Christ, everything seemed to stay the same. He sensed that he and his gang were lost, and that I wasn't. He wanted so much to give the Lord a chance and also to see his buddies follow the example he observed in Dean and me, but everything seemed so impossible. He felt just the way *I* had felt, that he had to escape somehow! Only for

Ricky the "way out" had been shooting dope with Frankie . . . mugging people in the streets . . . breaking into apartments . . . the whole bit.

These were the situations, and the people, who pressured me as I groped my own way toward identity. I was walking the streets all day, running the apartment, and taking twelve hours' credit at New York University, and I was getting more confused by the minute. What brought me up short was the blunt statement of a counselor: "Milliken, I think you're going to college because you're afraid."

I boiled. How dared this guy, safe in his ivy hall, say that to me when I rubbed elbows daily with danger and crises of the streets. "I haven't been afraid of *much*," I snapped.

The man gave me a level look. "You're afraid you won't be accepted by the people you want to have accept you—your Young Life people, your minister, your family, all the people with college degrees. You're afraid to be yourself, so you're just fighting through this education to prove something to them. Look, Milliken, you've proved yourself. You're killing yourself. Do you really want to go on? If you don't, be free enough, and man enough, to admit it."

That hit me where it hurt, but when I walked out of that office I felt as though a load had rolled off my back. The very next day I wrote letters to my Young Life superiors out in Colorado. I told them all simply that I wasn't going to be able to finish college, and I knew that a degree was required for Young Life staff people. It hurt to think of leaving them, but I was ready to clean streets for God if that was what He wanted me to do. I told them I just had to be myself, and I had to be free of everyone else's design for my life. They responded openly, and practically in unison, to the effect that "You're part of the staff. Don't sweat it. We want you!"

After that I was freed from the compulsions that I had to be what everybody expected. Freed from being forced into a middle-class value system, I began to see that God was bigger than man's traditions, that He could choose the direction suited to the individual capacities of the person He had made in the first place. I began to "Let go and let God," and when I began to be free, I began to relax. I had never had a "quiet time" before. Oh, I had pretended that I had; I had talked to people about it, and had even gotten kids off the streets to start regular Bible reading. But I myself couldn't sit down and read for more than five minutes—it was impossible for me to sit still that long. Now, as I began to be myself, I started loving the Scriptures; I could grasp the meaning for my life, and my situation. A new discipline began to take shape in my life.

The most humbling thing during this early stage in New York was the question that hit me at different times: "Could God possibly have brought me into the Inner City to change *me?*" At first, I didn't want to face this. I thought I was here to help the slum people. Could God possibly be bringing me to them so that *I* could be changed? When I began to consider this question, a whole new realm of God's love opened up. Could God love me this much? Could He care this much about my life? Would He go to the trouble of moving me all over the place—let me hurt, and be hurt; make mistakes, and have victories—in order to make me into the person He wanted me to be? I didn't want to face that either—the idea that God could care that much about me. It was hard. It's still hard.

Little by little I started to understand the profound truths behind the old clichés: "Jesus loves you as an individual. He cares for *you* as an individual." Suddenly it hit me—He died for *me!* He really loves *me*. And when Jesus Christ was here on earth He wasn't just dying for me at that moment; He was dying to a total commitment to my life, from the day I was born anew in Him, forever and ever. His commitment to me is twenty-four hours a day, forever!

I knew very well how much trouble I was having, living with the sin of the people on the streets for just a few hours at a time. And yet I began to see how He lives with me twenty-four hours of every day—with my thoughts, my motives, my childishness. *I* couldn't be easy for *Him* to take, yet He never tried to "escape." This gave me the perspective I needed. I got tough with my own self-pity. I learned to say to myself "What are you crying about, Milliken? What are you upset about? What great sacrifice are *you* making?"

Maybe during those lonely years it was necessary for me to pretend I was something I wasn't. Maybe I wouldn't have made it otherwise. I had to outpsych somebody. If I couldn't outpsych the guys on the street, I had to outpsych myself. Often our affluent society conditions us to avoid pain, to avoid suffering! As little children, we're taught that suffering is bad: "Here, keep this inside. It's bad. Keep this front that looks good. Look happy, even if all hell's going on inside." In the inner city the street kid doesn't play around with his feelings. He isn't going to put on that kind of front.

Oh, the street kid, I learned, has ways of hiding things all right. But if he's got an attitude, he's got an attitude, and his silence speaks so loudly that everybody around him knows it's there, too. As I lived on the street, this kind of transparency began to speak to me. Here I was, a suburban newcomer, pretending I was a nice little Christian. And the street kids were just plain honest about how they felt. They didn't want anything to do with me because I was a white man, and I don't blame them. If I had been they, I wouldn't have wanted a white man around my neighborhood, either. But I was there because I was convinced God wanted me there. I didn't know any other reason.

I was beginning to realize that slums creep into cities because of human negligence. The realization began to grow inside of me that millions of people are trapped in the tenements of the world, and that the vast middle classes have just let these conditions exist. And not only have they allowed them to exist, but to a great extent they have put walls around the ghettos to lessen a possibility of escape, or of change from within!

This is what the streets were saying to me: Suffering is a part of life; without suffering, you can't know life. In our society we go to such great lengths to be happy and escape suffering, or to deny suffering, and we miss out on so much as a result. When we live in the city and never get into the streets, we miss the fine gold. When we ride on the nice roads over the top of the city and say, "I must do something for those poor people down there," we not only miss the mire, and the things that are not so comfortable to look at, we also miss the beauty. We protect ourselves—we build a turtle shell around us, not just against the dirt and evil of the ghetto but against anything unpleasant.

Whenever we build this kind of shell around ourselves, and it doesn't get ripped away, we pay a price for living inside. We may think we are buying security—"I've got my home. I've got my picket fence. I've got my church. I've got my income." We have these advantages outwardly, and as long as we stay in our shell we are invulnerable to material threat. But inwardly we have paid a stiff sacrifice for our comfort. We have shut ourselves off from the type of hurt that produces love, the type of growth that builds manliness.

When I discovered the city ripping off my shell, I was embarrassed to see how skinny I was—as naked and funny-looking as a turtle that had lost its shell. I wasn't nearly so muscular as I had thought. But without the big shell of society, which I had seen and felt all around me, I discovered another shell of my own making.

Because this exposure in the city made me insecure, I shrugged deeper and deeper into my private shell. I wasn't unique in this. Lots of kids come to the Village from upper- and middle-class communities, in rebellion against the shell which their society has built around them. After they leave home they discover they have nothing within themselves to fall back on; they have that "naked" feeling, so they just build up a different shell.

For hours each week, while I was trying to escape my own nakedness, I sat in a tiny cafe in the Village, talking with other rebels, escaping the problems we found all around us. Slowly it became apparent to me that all we were doing in our rebellion was taking on a new-shaped, new-colored shell. At first this looked like freedom because we were free to let our hair grow, free to stay out all night, free to come and go as we pleased. Nobody cared what we did. But this wasn't really freedom; it was just a new shell to fit the new habitat. Village habitués who are smart enough soon see this. Some of the most creative people come out of this type of situation because they are able to pull themselves out of this preliminary deception and break the new shell in some healthy way. Others just sit down in the cafes, in the parks, on the stoops, and die inside. They haven't gained any real freedom. They walk around without any form, no way to go; and everywhere they turn they bump into the real question: "*Who am I?*"

It's no wonder there's an increase in the use of marijuana, no wonder the LSD trip has become so popular, no wonder the psychedelic experience calls out to a generation hungry for inner space. You have to resort to escape patterns when you have rebelled against tradition but have nothing else to fall back on or become part of. When a kid rebels and doesn't find anything to put his rebellion in, all of a sudden he knows he's trapped: "Here I am. But I'm still not me. I'm not really free. What do I do now?"

The exciting potential of a Christian's rebellion comes in the fact that he *has* a form, a direction, a purpose outside himself. I would like to see more Christian youth rebelling against the non-essentials, so they can be freed to truly find themelves, and to be remolded in Christ's way. This is what Paul was saying when he told the Romans not to conform to this world, but to be transformed by the renewing of their minds.

Often, instead of going through the pain of finding themselves, Christian young people end up going into a nice little Christian shell—they are taught to conform to a comfortable protectiveness: "Here's my little group. I'm pure and safe in here. The world's all wrong. Let's not get mixed up with it." Lots of people come into the church because they have rebelled against the world in the wrong way. They build up a nice little shrine around their new fellowship and say, in effect, "Naughty, naughty world! Nice, nice us!" Then they have to play a game of being as nice as people think they are, and they become defensive of themselves and critical of others. This destroys them inside, leaving them hollow and brittle. And non-Christians who see through them say, as I once did, that church members are hypocrites.

One of my favorite stories is the parable of the Prodigal Son. Any rebel, I've learned, is such a prodigal. In any culture, when we leave our society's shell we leave "the father," and at first it's great. "Whoopee! I've rebelled. I'm free." We head down the road, going some place but not knowing where, and when we get there we're in a pigpen. It's the "same old same old," as one of the coolest sayings on the street puts it!

"Here's a new idea," we say. "Let's go, let's follow it, let's break loose." And we end up back in the same old pen--still ourselves, still in the same society, and still having to live with it. It's like my experience of losing myself in that movie and feeling like a Spartan, but coming out to face the fact that I'm not a Spartan, I'm Bill Milliken. We may find temporary escape that way, but the world outside is still the same. Where's the freedom?

What is freedom? It seems to me that's the basic question that I and the other rebels were missing. The prodigal found that freedom ultimately lay in obedience to the father's will—but he had to go through the pigpen to find it. And so, in a way, did I.

One hot, miserable night during that summer when I was searching for myself, it seemed as if all the kids we knew were in the apartment. I wasn't in the mood to enter into their experiences. I was further away from the Lord than I'd been any time that year. Everything was off balance. I didn't want to be used. I didn't want to think. I left the apartment and wandered down to the waterfront, just wanting to look at the water and to be alone. But I couldn't get away from the questions in my own brain, no matter how far I walked.

"How come You keep using me, Lord? I don't deserve it. I yell out at You. I curse. I struggle. You know what I'm like, Lord. I know what I'm like. And these people down here know a little of what I'm like. Yet You continue to use me. Why?"

By the time I was through walking, the sun was shining and

I was exhausted—I had walked clear around Manhattan Island! I went back to the empty apartment—in summer nobody comes around during the day because the place is so stuffy—and fell asleep. It was not the first such experience I had that year, and it was not the last. I could understand, only too well, Ricky Rosario's dismay at discovering that accepting Christ doesn't mean the end of struggling. But I couldn't yet understand why God let things be that way.

A ghetto society is so exposed. The city can either destroy you or make you healthy. It's a real crucible; you can't just come to the city and get involved with people and be stagnant. I learned that those words in the Scripture about living *in* the world but not *of* it don't mean setting yourself up in a little cocoon.

Now, looking back, I can see that God was shoving us right smack into the middle of the world in order to teach us something. With the phone ringing and the buzzer buzzing, and a kid vomiting from an overdose, the tragedy of life hurt and racked us, but we began to find a vertical relationship with the Father which brought peace and stability within. We began to move *through* the frustration and corruption *to* the real freedom that comes in being obedient to His will. In that kind of freedom you can say, "You're hurting me, and I love you. I want to be involved with you; I'm right in the middle with you."

You cry out, but you can always come back to your knees. And your purpose, your desire, your goal is Christ. You can be involved in *anything*—because you have real freedom inside.

4

215 Madison

The times at 215 Madison were traumatic. We were facing dishonesty in some people who had always been honest with us; seeing them come along a little, then fall back again and disappoint us; having our clothes stolen, and knowing it was somebody in the building who was doing it. These guys undressed all our insecurities and our middle-class sharpness. Previously we had been able to handle a lot of our emotion by holding it in until we could get home by ourselves. Now our disappointments and hurts had to be suffered in the open. It was a spiritual strip-tease, and under the constant exposure I found myself falling apart.

At one point, a series of thefts from the apartments was having a bad effect on everyone in the building. One night, when we were all having supper at St. Chris', where we could get a balanced meal for a dollar, José walked out before dessert. We thought nothing of this, because leaving supper early was not unusual. When we got home much later, our television set was missing. That television set had been a very important part of our apartment set-up.

Checking things out, we found the back window open and one sneaker mark on the window sill. It was a very narrow clue, but I had the impression that José had been wearing sneakers. Both José and his buddy Manny were drug users, but José had gone through some changes and had come back to us at the apartment because he wanted another chance to prove himself. When we found José that night, his sole print matched the one on the window sill. Neither he nor Manny would say a thing.

With the whole morale of the apartment at stake, we had only one recourse. Dean and I drove them separately over to the precinct house. Both had records; both were on parole. During the very last block of the ride, both admitted they had stolen the TV. They asked us to forgive them and let them go. We forgave them, but we had a tough decision to make. We took them into the station where the situation became even more difficult when we encountered a new, young detective who was quite idealistic. In front of José and Manny he suggested that since we were working with the boys we should drop the charges. But Dean and I both felt this would be the wrong thing for us to do in this particular case. As a result, the boys were both put in prison for three years.

Some time later Dean got a letter from José thanking him for being tough with them. This was one of the harder things we had to do. Often the legal system takes such decisions out of our hands, but that time the choice was left squarely up to us and we had to make it.

On the other hand, there was the night when two of our Spanish kids got picked up for mugging a Chinese fellow from the neighborhood. I *knew* those two kids wouldn't hurt a fly. I accompanied the boys to court, and I became furious when the Chinese identified them as the ones who beat him up. I would have staked my life that this was a false accusation—so I asked the court for time, and I got it.

When you've been around our part of town, you get to know the system. You can sense which kids would mug, and which ones would not. You get to know things like this because you're a part of the fabric of the society, and here's where the difference shows up between coming into a neighborhood to work a few hours a day, and living there all the time. You pick up the vibrations; you know what's going on. This particular mugging looked to me like the work of somebody on drugs. Eventually, through the grapevine, I found out who the real muggers were. The street nearly always knows the identities in things like this, and if you work at it hard enough you learn where to be, or where to pick up a telephone at the right time, to find the answers. Then you make the connection.

When I located one of the muggers, I talked with him from three in the morning until sunup—told him how lousy it was to let these other guys take the rap for him. He couldn't believe I knew all the stuff I did about him. Kids never can believe that. But he respected me because I was so ingrained in his society that I knew what was happening, and he cracked. For the first time in the history of the Fifth Precinct, a young man turned himself in.

In the apartment, we became keenly aware of the delinquent subculture. Dean was doing a good bit of reading to acquaint us with the theories, the technical definitions, of different kinds of deviant social behavior. Neither of us attempted to identify overly with the people in the apartment or on the street. Dean was a little older than the kids, and we both were mainly interested in the work we were there to do, so we just weren't on an identification kick as some young leaders are. A lot of workers come down here and feel they can't accomplish anything with kids if they haven't gotten drunk or smoked pot with them. Or they feel they have to speak the street vocabulary, or dress as the kids do, or do all the latest dances. We knew the kids appreciated our being tuned in to where they live, but we also sensed that when they felt we were trying too hard to become one of them—across the age hurdle, the class hurdle, the cultural hurdle—they were embarrassed for us. They let us know over and over again that they liked us best when we were just ourselves. That honesty was the key to our acceptance.

Dean's experience in the Army and the time he had spent with guys and girls with problems in different situations had prepared him for the sort of life we were getting into in the apartment. Often in the early days he took the part of the "hatchet man," while I was more able to understand the guys emotionally. Then, when I'd have a tough confrontation with one of them, Dean would be there to try to interpret, or to help the guy relate to his next move. When Dean let the hatchet fall, I'd be there to pick up the pieces. We balanced each other off, and this giving the fellows two different images to relate to was a helpful thing.

The small apartment community at 215 Madison began to draw people like flies. Young kids who were involved in brutalities, thefts, sex offenses, drugs, got the word that they would be accepted at 215 Madison, but they also knew we would take action with them. The word was out that we stood for a different world, we stood for a square world. They could feel in us a condemnation of brutalities and illegalities. They knew that in accepting their subculture we had not approved of all their values. I think they came to the apartment because they appreciated this in us. Perhaps there is a strong compulsion toward discipline in these guys who have no father figure, who had not been dealt with in a strong way—either at home or in society. At any rate, we seemed to be providing a balance in the neighborhood.

We felt as if we were living in Grand Central Station. The apartment was a place to come and talk, to find friendship. From the beginning, Dean pushed the idea of the apartment as a substitute for the family, which so often is a weak unit in the ghetto. Ideally, it could become a place where an individual could struggle through emotional development that was missed at home.

We decided that as other apartments in the tenement building became available we would acquire them so we could increase the chances for more guys who "wanted to make it." We began to charge rent, depending on how much an individual could afford. Each person would have to maintain himself, since we had so little money, and this gave them more responsibility and self-respect anyway. Some others soon joined us, Little Eddy and José and Cisco and Trini and Butchie. Then there was Wayout Willie, and Dwight and Ollie and Mike. They were all equal on the ladder, which gave them a good feeling of security. We could encourage each other, borrow clothes, share food, go bowling or to church or to the movies together. We were developing a genuine alliance because we were living together and we were concerned about each other. Probably the biggest asset of all, beyond the group feeling we were developing, was the sense that we were going somewhere. We eventually made it a rule that our residents had to be either going to school or working. This gave everybody a goal, at least; everybody was really trying.

The basic problem for us was how to handle young adults, mostly in the 18-23 age group, *as* adults, while at the same time helping them through adolescent, if not infantile, stages of emotional development. It was not long until we began to see that this living arrangement had to be temporary; the apartment could not be a permanent home for the guys. It was a little of the "half-way house," which meant a fellow would have six months to a year, at the most two years, in which to go through several years of emotional growth. This was a rather delicate thing, but those who profited seemed to do so because there were other people in the apartment with similar problems. It was also necessary for us to expose our problems to them, which put us, too, in a vulnerable position, but through this kind of give and take we were able to lead them along.

It became apparent to us that the person who is failing in life senses this failure deep down inside himself, and that it acts as a weakening force throughout his whole personality. It almost castrates him—but he's forced to live with it. Dean began to see that these guys who were hanging out at 215 Madison had so rationalized their way of life that they made failure a norm. "A guy no longer thinks in terms of failure," he told me one night. "He thinks only in terms of his own norm." We began to talk together about how other possibilities do not exist for him, because they don't fit this norm. Occasionally we stumbled onto exciting insights into what else was happening. Through the friendships developing around the apartment, some of the guys were beginning to see areas in which they could expand their norm, or lift it. But in accomplishing this they went through repeated failures. The great thing about the situation at 215 was the fact that a fellow had companionship and friendship in his failure. Because of this he could move through his failure to success.

Through our involvement with the guys in the apartment, we gradually developed a positive philosophy regarding failure—that often it is only out of failure that success can come. We were learning that it is necessary to prepare a person to fail, to point him to success via failure. In the attempt to move from the smaller world to the larger world, and especially from hang-ups like drugs, a person has to meet situations that are too big for him to handle, and in those situations he will fail and adjust himself to failure. We found it was necessary to learn a positive attitude toward failure before a person could say, "I'm going to accept myself as I learn and as I fail."

We needed extreme sensitivity, knowing when to shove a guy a little bit, when to let him go, when to get rough. The tough side of love is so missing in many relationships. It's easy when you can put your arm around a guy and say, "You're wonderful." But telling a kid, "OK, it's time you grew up; I don't want to hear any more whining," is not easy. When a kid would get high, we wouldn't throw him out, but our standards were explicit that the use of drugs would put a fellow out of the apartment. It was always understood that there could be one, or two, or possibly more failures, which they would have to admit clearly and talk over with us. These would be warnings; but as soon as we sensed that in any way they were giving in to failure, they would be put out. It hurts to say, "You made a promise and you broke it. You're out on your own, and I'm not going to feel sorry for you. You're just finding excuses, and I don't care how many stories you give me. You get out; and when you're ready to come back, you come back."

We met together once a week for a time of counseling, hashing over what everybody was doing, getting our debilitating failures out in the open. Sometimes we had Bible studies with the whole group, and other times we met with members individually. In the group there was a freedom for fringe interest, which was important. Some of the fellows would lie on the bunks, half listening. We didn't put any pressure on them. But very often the prayer times that finished off these sessions were the most meaningful part of the week. This was what really cemented the group together in love.

The tough side of love is particularly necessary among kids who have grown up in a strongly matriarchal society without a strong male image. Too much freedom, coupled with a one-sided, overly-protective mother love, forms fertile ground for dishonesty, indifference, disrespect. Dean and I had to earn the closeness in our relationships with Frankie, with Ricky, with Eddie and Tap, and all the guys; the right at some point to step in as a father must and say, "I don't care how this makes you feel toward me. You may hate my guts; but I love you, and I'm doing this because I love you. I don't expect you'll understand right now, but I have to do it anyway."

When we were too afraid to be tough, we usually lost the kid; and there were many times when we hurt him by being too careful. We had to build the relationship first; we had to have him close to us. Paul Tournier talks about "that place": First of all, you give him "that place," but after you've done that you have to help him launch out from it. Some of the fellows completely rebelled against us at that point, others just faded away. Turning them out on their own, when you know it's the right move, is the hardest thing for an adult—parent or otherwise—to do, because you love them, and you don't want to see them mess up.

We learned this first through Rick. He flunked out a lot of times there at the apartment, and he came back and came back. Then finally, at one of the house meetings, he would not be honest with us about something. So we voted, and told him, "If you're willing to get honest with us, you stay. If you won't, you'll have to go." About ten minutes later he threw the keys at me. It was raining, so I drove him to Brooklyn where his mother lived. As we drove across Brooklyn Bridge he said, "Let me out here."

I felt sick. This guy was so intelligent, I had pinned my hopes on his making it—and here he was blowing it. "Rick, what are you going to do?" I asked.

"I don't know. Maybe I'll jump off this bridge."

He got out of the car, and vanished. As I drove away I knew I had to let him go even though my insides were aching. For three months he was gone from the neighborhood, and I had no idea what he had done. Then one day he came up to the door and said, "Bill, I'm ready to go!" He had made a deal with the Army; when they had seen his "tracks" from heroin injections, they had told him they couldn't take him, but he had convinced them that if he could stay clean for one year he could come back and enlist. He moved back into the apartment with us, he stayed off drugs entirely, the Army took him, and he became first in his platoon.

Ricky had had two years of people babying him, giving him support. He had to have that support as an individual, but he had to have the toughness to explode against. When he got that, he hit his turning point. He had to go off and do the rest with God. When he left, he was rebelling against God and us; I don't think he had the two quite separated. During the time away, he got them clarified. He realized that Dean and I were human, that we made mistakes; he found out that God was his Boss, that He was the one who would be with him all his life, not Bill or Dean.

This being tossed out and coming back again is a graphic example of how growth takes place. People from those early days are still coming back to us, and when they return they come at a different level from the one at which they left, even though they themselves may not be able to see it. It is our duty to interpret this to them and to say, for instance, "Ricky, you may think you're coming back after this defeat on a lower level, but in fact you're coming back at one higher up, because you've had the opportunity to fail, to live with your own defeat, to see its consequences, to experience our accepting you back. In coming back, you come on a higher level of maturity than when you went out."

The fact of living in the consequences of failure, gaining a larger perspective of oneself, seeing hope in a more mature way, enables a person to come back realizing that he and others can accept him even when he fails. This becomes a very important thing to remember.

The apartment was becoming a symbol of hope to the community. It spelled out a different style of life for those who came to live there, and to those who were not even in it the apartment spelled concern and a positive direction in which to move. Since then, we have been able to see how positively it interprets all this to the community, and at the same time identifies the Young Life program and leaders with the community in a visible way. Incidentally—and I think it should *be* incidentally—it solves some very practical and terrible problems for individuals who are suddenly homeless. One of the dangers of resident apartments is that they move to the level of being primarily practical expedients for the homeless. This cheapens the whole concept, and weakens it, and introduces all kinds of problems. To have the government throw up a housing unit, for example, for young teen-agers who are suddenly homeless, would probably be a tragedy. And this is what resident apartments can become without strong leadership.

We are dealing with young people who have not had a strong male image, and with women who have either given up or who are heroically trying—often without adequate support—and who, in compensating for this, are indulging, pitying, or nagging their children. Most of the guys are damaged by this very difficult kind of home problem. At its best the apartment needs to function in such a way as to provide an image of family, of friendship, and of a father.

5

The Cross Carriers

The Young Dragons were the main focus of my attention. We had gone to the beach together, played stickball, shot baskets in the gym, sat on benches in the park and talked for hours. Always we were trying to get the guys into some constructive activity, so they could begin to see some value in themselves. We were meeting with guys individually to study the Scripture, and to talk over problems, and we were available night and day, but one after another we saw the Young Dragons who had come to Christ slipping away, throwing over the faith that had lifted them so beautifully for a while. The days and nights were miserable as we watched every single kid we had brought to the Lord go back to the benches, back to prison, drugs, alcohol, everything. Seventeen hours a day for more than two years—I'd done little but concentrate on this gang, and every one of them went back to what he had been before. It looked as if everything was going down the drain.

I struggled with the problem in my mind. What was I doing wrong? Why was this happening? The pressures, the frustrations, and the questions built up. One day I was sitting in the apartment talking to Harv Oostdyk and two businessmen he had brought down to visit, and suddenly I just jumped up and ran from the room. All the way down to the docks I ran, and I was crying. I didn't know what I was crying about, but I couldn't stop. As I walked along the docks I suddenly had this overwhelming sense that I didn't know anything about love, that God's love was not coming through me to these kids I was trying so hard to reach. I heard myself crying out, "God, break me!"

During the next few months, one thing after another seemed to happen. I had no money. I became more and more discouraged. One morning I awoke with a stabbing pain in my stomach. I wound up in the hospital for X rays and tests. I had never experienced illness like this before. My stomach could tolerate nothing but milk; I slept eleven hours a day, and still woke up tired. I was depressed and confused, and I didn't even care whether I lived or died. The Oostdyks took me into their own home, and Emmy nursed me as if I were a brother.

It was hard for me to believe all this was happening to me. I had prayed to be broken—but this wasn't at all what I had had in mind! I didn't realize how egotistical I had been, or how many problems I had that needed breaking open. The new confidence I had slowly gained through my friendships with kids was smashed to nothing now. I quit speaking to the group, quit leading Bible studies, quit on everything. I didn't even have the confidence that I could have sold pencils on a street corner. The only thing I did was to sit in that apartment and listen to kids' problems. I wasn't any help to anybody, except maybe as a sounding board. And most days I didn't even want to listen.

That was the situation on one dismal, rainy day when Frankie walked in. I was sitting there depressed and feeling sorry for myself. Frank didn't have a smile on his face; his head was down. I knew immediately that he was hurting inside, but I just wanted to avoid him. I did not want to get involved with anybody else's discouragement or defeat. I sat there and looked at him for a whole minute, which seemed like an hour, before I could speak.

"OK, what's bugging you?"

Frankie looked me straight in the eye, and said between clenched teeth, "As far as I'm concerned, you and God and Jesus Christ can all go to hell!"

At that moment something exploded inside me. I grabbed him and threw him against the door, yelling, "Get out of here!"

Then, for the second time in a matter of months, I broke down and cried. I threw myself on the bed after he left, and then, on my knees, I began to analyze why I was crying. Was it because he had hurt me? He hadn't really; my insides had gotten pretty hard. Rather, it was because I loved Frank, and I had a sense of something tragic happening to him. My thinking became the clearest it had ever been, and I began to thank God. The thing that so excited me in the ebb tide of that explosion was the clear revelation that I loved this guy. There was no light shining from heaven, or angels hovering around me, but the message came through loud and clear: My whole work for the first two years had been centered around Bill Milliken instead of Jesus Christ. That's why kids were dropping away all the time. It wasn't the fact that God was weak, or that He couldn't work in this kind of society. It was just that I had built up the whole work around myself!

When Dean came home I talked the whole thing over with him. During the next few days we talked and prayed by the hour. I had never prayed like that before, and I have never quite been able to again—just hours of turning myself and everything else over to God, the humble confession of saying, "I can't run it, Lord. I quit. You have to take over."

The change was almost immediate. I graduated from milk to baby food; I quit taking pills; I forgot I had an ulcer. My mind was obsessed with a new idea. None of the guys could make the grade alone, on a separate basis, as an individual. We all needed each other—including Milliken! Here God was giving me the answer, not only to the need of my young friends, but to my own need as well. I had been trying to meet with each fellow individually, helping him study the Bible and pray. But I began to see that as long as we were fighting our spiritual battles only as individuals, we became easy prey for the strong forces of evil all around us. It made sense that if a gang broke up because certain members had met Christ, those guys needed another structure, equally as solid as the gang, to meet their new needs.

I had to start building from the bottom. I talked to a bunch of the guys, and Clark Jones and four of the Puerto Rican fellows agreed at least to try something different. I told them, "It'll be the hardest thing we've ever done."

The first time we met in the apartment I confessed, "I don't even know what I believe any more, but I know I need you guys. If Christ is real, then let's go all out. I have problems like you. I hurt. I hate. I lust. But let's get to know each other. Let's learn to love. Let's hang in there together and make it. We can't be phony. We've got to go all the way or not at all. It won't work any other way.

"If Christ isn't real, then I'll go back to Pittsburgh and get a job in the family brick company. I'll make money and live it up. The hell with everyone else. But if He is real, let's give it everything."

One saying kept going through my mind—*If Jesus Christ be God, and died for me, then no sacrifice I make for Him is too great.* And the words of Christ, too, that said anyone who wanted to go with Him must forget himself, and take up his cross every day, and follow Him. We decided to call ourselves the Cross Carriers, and see what would happen.

Those were hard days, but we began to build a solid community of love. At first it was rough trying to be honest, even with ourselves. There was so much we needed to get out of us! It reminded me of the time when I had had a boil on my hand, and missed a wrestling match because I didn't have it taken care of correctly. All I had to do was get it lanced, but instead I had put on some salve and bandages, which didn't get to the heart of the infection.

We began to see that that was what we had been doing lots of times with our problems—putting some nice salve and a lot of white bandages on the outside, instead of getting into the heart of our troubles. Gradually we developed a format for the group. We would open with prayer, then I would go around the circle and tell each person his weak spots. Then I would go around again, building them up by pointing out areas where I had seen personal progress. Pretty soon one of the guys would start in on me—after a while they got so they could really slam me into place. Then we would have a time of confession. This was rough; it was a whole new way of life. Many times someone would blow up and run out, because he had been hurt, or because he knew someone else was not being honest.

Some of our meetings would get real hot. It was not uncommon for a guy to go away and not show up the following week—but he almost always came back eventually. Even in my Young Life Campaigner group back in high school I'd had that same feeling of not wanting to go near those Christians if I'd done something I knew was wrong—particularly if it had gotten around and there was gossip. I just didn't want to be around that leader if my conscience was hurting.

What I was trying to pound into the Cross Carriers from the very beginning was that *you need the group more than ever when you have failed*. And the group has to have enough love to allow the individual to fail without gossiping about him or calling him a hypocrite—and without thinking itself too "good" to associate with him. When a person sins here in the city, the rest of the Christians don't start falling away. Oh, they did at first, but that was because I had inflicted my own middle class mores on them; once I let them be themselves, a stark honesty took over. We were able to say to each other, "Come on, we'll pick you up. Let's go!" That's why Cross Carriers was able to take off.

In the early days of the Cross Carriers, the six guys looked to me as their leader. But gradually they began to accept the fact that I too had faults, and needs, and problems. I'll never forget the day I was talking to them about drinking in the park. When I was all through, Clark looked at me and said quietly, "Well, Bill, you do some things we don't think are right either."

God was uncovering a lot of failure mechanisms in all of us—bad attitudes, bad motives, defensive emotion. But hidden away in the mire of ourselves, and of the ghetto, lay a wealth of gold. We were finding that if we were willing to pay the price, to put up with living right in the middle of the mire, that we were able to see beyond the mire to the gold. And whenever that gold gleamed, it took us aback—it was a humbling, yet explosive experience. When you dig deep, you hit hard rock. But in order to get the gold you have to dig deeper still. You have to pay a price for real gold.

When you dare to move out into the middle of life, Christ allows an explosion of love to take place between people. Soon the trust builds up between you, and you are not afraid to explode and let the badness out. Through the explosion, you come alive in a new way, and you're free. It's like that boil I had—you can keep the sickness inside if you choose to, but it affects your attitude, your activity, your health. We had been keeping the weakness, the resentment, the envy, the anger inside us, all covered up. The sickness was there, just the same, and it needed to have the antidote of Christ's love applied to it day after day. We began to find out, in the group, that we could expose the hurt and sensitivity that welled up inside us to the healing of Christ through our community of love. As we became healed, we were undergoing something of the process of becoming disciples.

With some people who don't know how to give or to receive friendship, you just keep giving and giving to them. The more you give, the more the pressure builds until the explosion finally takes place and the two of you make contact. Personally, I am always looking for that point of contact with a person, that place where we begin to communicate. You jab at it, you work at it, always looking for the place that is sensitive to him, that place where he really lives. When you find it, there's often an explosion, but this clears the air for deepening friendship in a way that cannot take place otherwise.

Another kind of explosion takes place with the hostile person, the one who doesn't want anything to do with you. Maybe he has gotten up enough nerve to taunt you, or your love and concern has bugged him to reaction. It really bothers him that you keep caring about him, and he'll find some reason to take a jab at you. Deep down he may really want to trust you, but there's so much hate and bitterness there that he can't break through till this explosion. At times like that I throw a few quick jabs myself while I have a chance, and I pray my hardest for God's wisdom. If you jab wrong you can close a person off even deeper, but if you get the right licks in you reach the heart, and there's real dialogue, and often you'll be able to find the spot again later and open it even wider.

An explosion isn't always a yelling, screaming type of thing; it may be a weeping. All of a sudden a light goes on—one person may get mad; another sees his sin; someone else sees he's been held down, and the world suddenly gets bigger. Whatever form it finds, it usually takes place because for the first time the person feels love. The bad feelings settle steadily, throwing poison throughout a person's entire system. Only love can draw out the infections of the soul. This is part of why we need to be loved—to have the pollution drained out of our lives.

Finding our place here in the city wasn't at all the "Here's the big God coming in" sort of thing, or the "Wonderful Christian with all the answers." It was a coming to the realization that we did bring some important gifts stemming from our different heritage. The biggest thing we discovered was that we had to come open and willing to learn ourselves, willing for God to do with us what He wanted. In the process we were stumbling across the beauty of the people in the city. God had already been at work in them, and He was just waiting to bring them together with this other element He had prepared out in the suburbs. When He got the two together, the explosion took place and we both learned. Instead of a vertical relationship ("Here, come up to my level!"), there was a horizontal relationship developing, with each of us nurturing the other. They were teaching us the beauty of their freedom and openness; we brought the knowledge and disciplines of our suburban heritage. And with the blending of the two elements we were able to help each other grow in Christ.

As the smoke of the explosion cleared we were always amazed at the fantastic potential and beauty of the inner city person.

6

Bobo, My Friend

ONE PERSON, more than any other, taught me this truth about the potential, and the strength and dignity, that lie beneath the surface of the inner city. He is Robert Nixon—Bobo, my friend.

Bobo started life down in the South Carolina country where he lived with his grandmother two miles away from the school. Every day, scared to death, he would run home those two miles with the big kids chasing him all the way. His mother was in New York working in a textile factory; his father, away in the Navy, seldom showed up; the fear inside Bobo pounded with no outlet. His grandmother never allowed any of the kids to come into the house crying—she would turn them around and send them out to face whatever enemy had caused the tears. Eventually an uncle threatened to beat Bobo if he ran away from "those guys" one more time. Bobo was cornered. The next day, mindful of his uncle's threat, he turned around and slugged the fellow who was chasing him. To the surprise of both, Bobo won! That happened in second grade. For years after that, Bobo hardly ever stopped fighting.

When he was nine, his grandmother entered the hospital for surgery and, expecting to die, sent the five grandchildren to live with their mother in Harlem. The very first time Bobo went out to play in 114th Street, he got into a fight. All that first year he fought, until his mother decided to move to an entirely new neighborhood where Bobo could start over clean.

They settled into an apartment on the Lower East Side. Inevitably, a new conflict turned up—in the person of Butch. For two weeks, Bobo and Butch fought wherever they met. Finally Butch gave up, and as soon as he accepted Bobo's ability to beat him, all his friends in the neighborhood did too, and became Bobo's friends.

During that first year in New York City an incident occurred in school which filled Bobo with hatred. His teacher was a woman, and white, and her favorite pupil was a white boy who sat near her desk. One day Bobo noticed that he and this Georgie had pens just alike. That pen was such an important possession to Bobo that he can still see it vividly—gold-colored, the top covered with little colored rhinestones that shone like diamonds.

One day Georgie lost his pen. His eyes darted to Bobo's, and immediately he told the teacher that Bobo had stolen his pen. "Robert, give George his pen," the teacher demanded.

"It's not his," Bobo answered truthfully.

"Stealing's bad enough, but lying's worse," the teacher snapped. And she walked back to Bobo's desk, took the prized pen away from him, and handed it to Georgie.

All the way home that afternoon Bobo cried, and when he told his mother about the incident she advised him, "Just try to forget it. There's nothing you can do about some things in this life."

It wasn't long before Bobo and his brother Tap found out how to take care of the things "you can't do anything about." This was what gangs were for on the Lower East Side. The Nixon brothers moved into the Young Pagans to defend their rights. Bobo carried a hatchet at first, while most of the others had switchblades, zip guns, or real rifles stolen from pawnshops. These weapons were used regularly, and rough and tumble fights of earlier days gradually gave way to battles where blood was shed and death occasionally sobered the scene.

Bobo's capacity and desire for leadership moved him steadily upward in the gang structure until he became War Counselor, the officer in charge of stirring up fights; then vice president; and finally president. At one time he worked on war strategy with a guy named Stitch, who hated whites almost as much as he did. They got along fine, but The Man (as they called the police) was always on their backs, and Stitch was particularly violent with white policemen. Stitch was known all over the area because he had been in so many fights; his body was a mess of scars from knife wounds.

One day when Bobo was sitting on a park bench waiting for his girl friend, The Man came by and told him, "Move along."

Bobo answered, "I'm waiting for someone."

"Don't get wise, Sam," growled the cop. "I said move it."

Bobo didn't move, so the policeman grabbed him and started shoving. Bo shoved back, and before he knew what was happening the cop blew his whistle and another policeman arrived with a billyclub. A couple of raps with the club, and Bobo sprawled on the ground. The police were ready to take him in, but Bobo promised to go home if they would let him go. For some reason they turned him loose—and, unwittingly, turned all hell loose too! For two weeks after that Bobo's gang tossed garbage cans from the tenement roofs onto the cops walking their beats.

As a child, Bobo had felt the usual sense of being inferior to whites. When he was thirteen years old he thought Africa was the way Hollywood portrayed it—that there really was a cat named Tarzan who ran the jungle, who could do in twenty stupid-looking, half-naked black Africans single-handed. He didn't want to be associated with those Africans; they were stupid! But the kinds of things he thought about those Hollywood stereotypes he also applied to himself: "I'm stupid!"

Bobo took it for granted that everything worthwhile had been done by white people. It was a young black social worker named Bill Marshall who first introduced him to Afro-American history. Bobo got quite a start when he learned about Booker T. Washington, and Frederick Douglass, and others and found that the first doctor to operate successfully on the human heart was a black man from Chicago! He began to get a completely different image of himself and of his race. But as he developed confidence in himself, his hatred of the whites intensified.

Bill Marshall, who was proud of being black, created a thirst in Bobo and Tap and Eddie to be somebody. The era of the gangs was ending in New York now, in the late 'fifties and early 'sixties, and those three were among the first ex-gang members to start a social club because they had such a strong desire to do something with their lives. They and three friends organized the Big Six with Bill Marshall as their advisor. It became the key group in the Smith Project in the post-gang days. Each member had his own outstanding contribution to make to the group. Tap was the athlete, an outstanding basketball player; Eddie was the convincing spokesman and disciplinarian; Bobo was the hot-headed debater. Then there was Ken, the intellectual, and Ernie, the big lover who could always round up girls for their socials.

Each member of the Big Six was also responsible for developing an outside contact who could be useful. One of them got acquainted with a district attorney who lived in the project and was active in the local Little League. When the club had accumulated $60 clear, they decided to give it to a worthy cause, and after considering the Freedom Marches or Africa, decided to put it locally into the Little League in order to help the younger kids who were coming along. The DA wrote back to thank them and to offer his help if they ever needed it. Right away, they made a request, and the attorney made it possible for one of their guys to be released from prison.

Some of the money they raised through their social affairs was earmarked for Big Six sweaters, but the guys got tired of waiting for the treasurer to announce there was enough money available. When they investigated the situation, they found out he had been using the money for his own fun! After that they clamped down and made some very strict rules. The Big Six was a real boss outfit—they followed parliamentary procedure, mailed out post-card reminders and copies of the minutes each week, dressed up in shirts and ties for their meetings at St. Christopher's. It was a swinging club.

In and around St. Chris' was where I began to make contact with Eddie and Tap, but Bobo wouldn't have a thing to do with me. I had to bide my time with Bobo for a couple of years. I'd seen him in the park shortly after Eddie and Tap came back from Colorado, but it was obvious Bobo didn't want me playing basketball with them. He didn't like or trust me, and I was definitely at a disadvantage in being white.

Even after Eddie and Tap had come to accept me as an individual, Bobo still hated me. The three of them were in a rock 'n roll singing group, and I invited them to sing one evening at club over in St. Christopher's gym. Bobo didn't want to come to club, but the others overruled him and they all came. After they were through with their numbers, and I started to talk about Christ, Bobo walked out.

"I thought you had no right to be up there talking to me like that," he told me later. "I certainly didn't need church on a Monday night! Besides, it seemed the things you were saying were foreign there in the gym, because it wasn't in church." The next time I asked them to sing, Bobo hung around afterwards; he had discovered that a lot of people he knew came to club. By this time his brother Tap was a member of Cross Carriers, and he used to take home a lot of Bible verses to learn. He started having Bobo help him memorize them. Then Bobo began to come around regularly to Young Life club and I kept hanging around the parks where Bobo played ball. As I felt his hostility slowly breaking down, I decided to push it a little and ask him to come down and talk to me at 215, any time anything was bothering him. He wasn't ready. Bobo had been raised on the street, and everything he had learned was off the street, and he figured he could take care of himself and his own problems. More time passed, and I bumped into him here and there, and we talked occasionally on a friendly, casual basis. Tap invited me up for dinner once. Finally, one day I went directly to Bobo and told him I wanted to meet him at 215 in half an hour.

I was standing at the refrigerator when he walked in. Here were the two of us, guys who had nothing at all in common, one of whom actually disliked the other. I poured him a glass of orange juice and tilted the bottle to finish off the last few swallows myself, and we started talking. I told him a little about my family, and the years when I was growing up in Pittsburgh. I shared some of my deep feelings about fear and rejection and inferiority and hatred. This gave him the opening to pull out some of the things that were bothering him. He was very sensitive about his family's being broken up; he had a problem with his temper; he was always getting into fights. He talked about his hatred for white people and what had caused it. Then I told him about Christ and the difference He had made in my life. I told him he could have this same Christ if he wanted Him.

Later Bobo told me, "Nobody'd ever talked to me like that. It overwhelmed me. Even those guys on the street—the ones I called my best friends—didn't share their deep problems with me."

Bobo had been going to church on Sunday all his life; he had seen people come in all dressed up for a social gathering, and then he heard them fighting in their apartments after they went home again. He didn't want any part of that kind of Christianity, and he was skeptical about Jesus Christ.

After that talk, I had the feeling Bobo was spying on me. He watched me whenever our paths crossed—in the parks, around the community, at club. A lot of people come to the Lower East Side just to get something and then leave. College students come to write a paper on the "poor people" of the inner city; social workers come in for a year or two, just long enough for kids to get attached to them, and then move on. "I couldn't figure what your angle was," Bobo said later; "I didn't see the same kind of stuff I'd seen in other people. You had a nice place to live in Pittsburgh, and yet you said you were going to stay—as long as the Lord wanted you here."

The trust began to build up gradually. I remember another occasion when he was up in my apartment and I started telling him of the potential I could see in him. He had thought he was only capable of leading a bunch of guys into trouble, but I knew he could be a leader for Christ if he wanted to let Christ take over his life. He didn't know what I meant by "Let Christ take over." He had seen something in his brother and in Eddie when they came back from the ranch, but he hadn't wanted to ask them about it. I told him, "Bobo, either you can lead guys in hate, or you can lead them to try to change this neighborhood. Christ can give you the kind of strength to do that, and He can use leadership ability like yours."

I remember his saying, "I don't know what you want me to do, but if Christ can change me, then I'll give Him a chance."

After that we met secretly, just the two of us, because he wasn't ready to let the fellows know. As we studied and he learned more about who Christ is and what He does, he became more attracted to the whole idea of being His disciple. This was hard for Bobo because he was respected in the neighborhood as a tough guy, and now it seemed to him that Christ was calling him to love instead of hate.

We were always trying to encourage each other out of the weaknesses we had. Bobo had a particularly hard time with his temper. There were many times when he was all ready to smash a guy. It took him a while before he would admit that his temper was a weakness. "I can control it," he would say. But we all knew he couldn't. He was like an open book.

Finally Bobo came to the point where he admitted to all of us that his temper was something he could not control. It was hard for him to do. He even grew angry in admitting it to us, but this was the beginning of a change in him. Shortly after this admission, Bobo was out shooting baskets when a kid came up to him, took the ball, and threw it off the court. "Go get that ball," Bobo told him.

"No, I won't," the kid said, and he started cursing Bobo, really laying it to him. "You're a phony and I can beat you if I want to." Then he grabbed Bobo—and they just fought it out right there on the basketball court.

After the fight the kid was sitting on the bench, crying, and Bobo walked over to him and said, "Look! I'm sorry."

This was unheard of. Bobo never said he was sorry to anybody he fought.

Another time, as he was coming from the gym, he wanted to get through a crowd gathered on the sidewalk, so he just walked through, and somebody shoved him. Bobo wheeled around.

"OK," he said, "who did it?"

A guy stepped out of the crowd. "I did it. What are you gonna make of it?"

"Look" Bobo answered, "maybe we just had a misunderstanding. I'm sorry."

Everybody laughed, of course. Inside Bobo burned because he

knew these guys, and he knew he could beat any of them. But he gritted his teeth and walked away. After awhile, he learned by watching the rest of us that when something starts to bug you too much, at times you've got to laugh it off or the anger will control you. If you make a joke out of it instead of getting mad, it won't get you.

All these tests brought Bobo to the place where he really meant business with the Lord. "When I start something," he told me, "I want to go all the way. I'm either all out for it, or I won't try it at all."

Bobo was not yet in the Cross Carriers, for I'd been waiting until he indicated he wanted to be seriously committed to Christ. It was about a year after his first prayer that we invited him to join. "This was unheard of," he told me later, "my being invited *into* a group. I was never *out* of a group before; I was *always* in!"

None of the fellows quite realized at the time how much was happening to them as a result of their new life with Christ and with each other. One night when Bobo, Clark and Eddie were sharing some stuff about themselves—their frustrations and their progress—Bobo said, "Man! You guys are really making it!" This was after Clark and Eddie started school at Newark Prep, and they were working pretty hard. Sometimes they would study all night with no sleep at all, or they would set the alarm for the middle of the night in order to wake up and study. Bo was proud of them and felt like encouraging them. "Man! This is great! I really admire you guys."

At that point Eddie rolled over and said, "Something's happening to you, too, Bobo. You've been taking things that years ago you wouldn't have stood for."

Bobo lay on the bed and thought about that. Nobody knew him better than Eddie. For years they had hung around together. If a change was obvious to Eddie, then it was real. Eddie's observation made Bobo realize that Christ was laying hold of his temper. Any big change in a person—whether he's an alcoholic, or a junkie, or a fighter, or just plain self-centered—is going to be noticed. When Christ gets a hold of a life and begins to change it, people are going to see.

Bobo still has a struggle; he still catches an attitude, as the street puts it. He still flares up if he knows some guy is pushing his weight around. His temper didn't just vanish the way we wish our weaknesses would.

"I try to wait the thing out till my temper cools down," Bobo says. "Sometimes I have to walk away from the scene before it cools; then I try to go back and make an apology to the other person. After that I go to God with it. This is the only way I can feel right about any of my emotions. I think for me the first step has to be to the other person. This is what takes guts."

We were seeing a community of love bring Christ's healing power into our sickness. We could see God taking the raw materials we brought to Him, and remolding them for His use. This is so much the truth of the gospel: God doesn't want to take things away from our lives; He wants to *redirect* them for His creative purposes. He makes use of what we bring to Him when we let our wills be His will. For instance in my own life I have been a rebel. When Christ took over my life He did not stop me from being a rebel, but He redirected my rebellion to be used by Him for His cause.

This change was what was happening that year to Bobo—and to me. The Cross Carriers changed me far more than it did any of the kids. And as I changed, I could see so clearly the error in saying, "Come on up here where I am." All of us in the group were the same. Sure, we had different colored skins, we were conditioned differently—but we were the same inside. We learned to meet as peers, as people, rather than as a social worker with cases, or as a teacher with learners.

One day, when Bobo and I were talking together over lunch, we realized what had really happened to us. Our educational backgrounds were different, our houses were different, our parents were different, our lives were different. But when we started talking about what we were inside—the fear, the insecurity, the loneliness, the need to be accepted—we were the same. We were one—in Christ.

7

Tough Love

THROUGH all these guys—Clark and Tap, Bobo and Eddie—we felt the walls of the inner city begin to break open. The seeds of leadership had started to grow, the great things the Lord could do through them were becoming obvious. After the first year with the Cross Carriers we got forty kids to go with us to the Colorado ranch. That group has since come to be known as the "Phenomenal Forty." I have never seen a busload like that, before or since. It was a God-picked group—I am sure of that.

Out of the forty, I picked eight fellows I wanted to zero in on and put them in my cabin. Tap especially was very crucial to my planning. Our friendship had started to grow, and it was natural for me to look to him for cooperation during the trip. I guess I was expecting too much, because a little friction developed between us on the way out. Tap could get into terrible moods, especially when things didn't go his way. And he'd stay in a mood until things went the way he wanted. This time he was a little more aggressive about it than I'd seen him be before. At night we would go into the cabin, and I'd try to have a "cabin time," a few minutes before lights out to think seriously about life and talk over problems together. Tap and his friend Ronnie would do everything they could to mess it up. By the third night they were really getting to me, and all the guys were giving me a hard time in a lot of little ways. After the meeting, when the guys were in the cabin getting ready for bed, I pushed open the door and saw Ronnie just standing there.

"Time to hit the sack, Ronnie," I said.

"I'm not going to bed." He was sounding me. "I'm staying up all night!"

"Heck you are!" I saw the whole situation becoming a challenge. We started fooling around and wrestling, and I ended up throwing Ronnie into the closet and locking the door.

When Tap saw what had happened he stepped in on his buddy's side. "You better leave him out of that closet, Bill."

"Nothing doing," I said. "He's been giving me trouble every day since we got here. I mean business!"

About that time John came in and looked over the situation. "What's going on?" He joined Tap in trying to get the closet door open, and I was wrestling both of them, trying to keep them away from it. Just as they succeeded in forcing it open, Boot and another guy walked into the cabin. I didn't know where they stood, but they'd been having a little friction with the other guys so they jumped in on my side. It was still just fooling around, but I didn't know where it would end—it might stay friendly, or it could turn into a full-scale fight. I was wrestling Tap, Boot got Ronnie back into the closet, and all of a sudden my side had won.

Everybody got into bed, but pretty soon little testing noises started going back and forth from bunk to bunk. I sensed the tense feeling building up again, so I called out, "OK, guys, knock it off!"

Most of them did, but Tap muttered, "I ain't knockin' nothin' off!" This was the most aggression he'd ever shown toward me. "Nobody's going to sleep tonight." Then he started using foul language, and I told him to keep quiet or else.

"Or else what?"

This was a real challenge. Things were getting out of hand, and I knew it. I was pretty upset myself by this time, so I snapped, "OK, Tap! We're going to take our differences outside and settle them!"

This was a major goof on my part, but I didn't know what else to do. I'd been having trouble anyway in establishing myself as a leader of this group and in winning their respect. If I allowed myself to be backed down now from the firm position I'd taken, I'd have real chaos on my hands.

At the same time, though, I had put Tap in a position where

he couldn't back out either without looking like a chump. "OK," he said, "if we're going out, let's go."

One of the guys warned, "Tap, don't go out there! He's bigger than you." After that there wasn't a sound in that cabin. All you could see was eyes following us as we got out of bed and pulled on our pants.

"I'll meet you downstairs," I called back as I went out the door. The cabin was a two-decker one and Dean had several guys in with him on the lower level. As I passed his door I stuck my head in and said, "Guard that door and don't let anybody out. I don't want anyone else jumping in."

By the time I got outside into the night, I felt thoroughly sick. All I could think was, "Oh, man! If I fight him, what kind of a witness is this?" I stood there waiting for Tap and praying hard for wisdom.

When he came up to me, I turned to him with a challenge. "Tap, you know I'm not afraid of you. Maybe I'll get my behind kicked, and maybe I won't." Tap just stood there staring at me, his head kind of bobbing, and I continued, "I'm not afraid to fight you, but I would like to ask you a couple of questions first."

Then I really lit into him verbally, giving him every reason in the world to slug me in the mouth. I didn't yell, but I didn't spare him at all. "I thought you were a Christian, Tap. What an example you're setting! Man! I asked you to help me, and you've been the worst guy. I thought we were friends. Friends just don't treat each other this way."

I tore him right down to bottom, and then I started to build him back up. "There's probably nobody at this stage of the game who has more of a potential to pull guys in either direction. You're a basketball star, you've got a great singing group, everything's going for you. Man, what you could do for God if you let Him take over!" I stood back and waited. He said nothing. "Look, if you still want to fight, fine!" I waited again. Instead of slugging me, Tap suddenly broke down. He started talking, telling me his problems, and then he prayed and recommitted his life to Christ right there in the dark woods outside the cabin.

The really significant thing was the complete change in the

atmosphere the next day. Tap went to each one of those guys, and before bedtime everyone in my cabin had come up to me and apologized. Each one asked if we could talk together as a group.

It was so honest that night. Each guy told exactly what he was thinking: why he didn't believe in God; why he was acting up; what he didn't understand about the talks at the meetings. I told them what had happened in my own life—that someone had cared enough to make me look at God's plan, and that this was all I was asking them to do.

"You don't have to accept it," I assured them. "All I'm asking you to do is look at it. The main reason why I'm in the city is to give you as clear a picture as I can of the difference Christ can make in your life. If you don't want it, fine; I'm still your friend. We can go home and things will be the same as always. But I want you at least to love yourself enough to look at it. Be man enough to think seriously about it."

Very quickly I told them what to look for in the rest of the talks; then I prayed, and that was it for the night.

They did as I asked and from that time on, during the last three days of the camp, I had a chance to talk individually to every one of my eight guys, and every one of them decided to take God up on His offer.

That was a costly experience, another lesson in tough love—God's love in spite of myself when I didn't know what was right.

These were the kids that God had picked. After that trip the whole ministry began to fan out. I wasn't putting in any more time, neither was Dean, but we had added seven new Cross Carriers and there were more of us now to carry the load.

Personally, I was feeling better all the time. In fact, when I came back from Colorado I stopped off at my local draft board in Pittsburgh for my physical, and the next day or so they sent me a telegram, "Report for duty." The new X rays were completely negative! The doctors couldn't understand it. The pictures looked as though there had never been anything wrong in my stomach, and it appeared I would soon be on my way into the service. I appealed, and to my surprise the draft board gave me a 4-D classification, a ministerial deferment, even though I was not an ordained minister and hadn't even finished college. Just to see God's hand in this way, at that particular time, was so great! He was showing me again that if I could only be patient and wait, I'd be able to see Him and His plan for us all. It's funny that we never learn—or rather that we learn and then forget, and He has to teach us all over again!

We hadn't been able to interest Eddie in going to Colorado with us because he didn't want to hear any more about Christ. After we came back to the Lower East Side, Boot went over to the park and sat down on a bench next to Eddie. He told him what a great time he'd had, and how he had accepted Christ into his life. Ed knew Boot—they'd been pretty good friends up to this point. Ed also knew that Boot had gone out West to party, just as he himself had done the summer before. Now here was Boot back in New York telling him that he had accepted Christ and that his life was beginning to change. All Ed could feel as Boot talked was, "This is a lot of garbage!" because he had been through exactly the same feelings the year before. He said, "Yeah, Boot. That's nice. But look, in two or three months, you're not going to feel this way."

Near the end of summer, I took a chance with Ed Gist and sent him out to our Young Life College Prep Week. I told him the changing point in my own life had come through the conversations I had gotten into at College Prep, and that I wanted him to go and at least give it a try. Ed was surprised that anybody would stick with him after he had rejected everything. "If this made a difference in your life," he told me, "after you accepted Christ, then maybe it can make a difference in my life, too."

That week was the spark Ed needed. All through it he kept saying to the other kids, "No, I'm not a Christian, and I don't know what I believe about anything!" But the night before he came back to New York, Eddie and his counselor walked back from the meeting together and Ed admitted, "I really want to have a life with Christ, but I just don't know how it happens. I tried last year, and it didn't work."

They stopped walking as they passed a stump, and the counselor said, "Ed, sit on that stump." Ed sat down without knowing what the counselor had in mind. "It held you up, didn't it?"

"Yeah," Ed conceded.

"You know, your life with Christ has to be like that. You accept Christ and He holds you up. If you believe He is there with you in New York, He will hold you up. But you have to rest your whole weight on Him like you did on that stump."

When Ed came back to the streets from College Prep, things began to change. He wasn't even in high school, yet I had sensed he had the natural intelligence to communicate with those new college freshmen. And he had. They told us Ed added as much to the thinking that week as anyone else there. "What was different was me, I guess," Ed explained. From that point on, Ed began to grow steadily.

Clark and Eddie and Bobo moved into the same apartment some time after that. It was already obvious to us that coming into the Young Life apartments gave certain of the guys the assist they needed in the natural process of withdrawing from their home situations. It gave them new experience in living with other people, in learning how to cope with different attitudes and expectations, in the general task of growing up and of developing into persons.

Clark and Eddie were going to Newark Prep, and Bobo was working days and going to night school. They developed a real concern for each other. It showed up every morning. Clark and Eddie would set the alarm for 6:30, but Bobo didn't have to think about an early schedule, because he didn't leave for work until nine o'clock. Most mornings Clark would get up first, turn off the alarm, and head for the bathroom to wash up. That would take him about fifteen minutes during which Eddie lay in bed, loving those extra minutes of sack-time. Faithful, consistent Clark took the responsibility morning after morning, and Eddie got to depend on him to take the initiative.

Then one morning, after the guys had all been up late the night before, the alarm started to ring and nothing happened. Eddie lay there, expecting Clark to get up as usual, but apparently that morning Clark had decided, "To hell with you guys. Get up and turn it off yourselves!" Finally, it was Bobo who got up—and he didn't have to leave for work for three hours!

For about two weeks straight this same thing happened—Bobo would get up, turn off the alarm, and then wake Clark and Eddie. They were so impressed with his willingness to get up when he didn't have to, just to get them off to school on time, that they knew without Bobo's saying a word that he was concerned about them.

Whenever one of the guys ran into a problem he felt free to talk it over with the others; the fellows would listen and help find a solution. They lived together, worked together, and pushed and pulled each other toward their respective goals. Eddie would help Clark with his algebra, Clark would help Eddie with his English, and the other guys who were in school often came over to their apartment to study because they could concentrate on homework there in peace and quiet, most of the time. The strength of the group was an important aid in the successful progress individuals made toward their chosen goals. Each fellow needed to examine his life, to see where he was at the present moment, and to decide where he wanted to go from there. The apartment setup was proving a center of constructive learning, and a place where residents could experience great love for one another.

8

Red Roses and Peanut Butter

THERE's one facet of these guys' lives that I haven't mentioned yet—girls. The girls came to us inevitably because the guys were there. We saw them becoming a greater part of our lives all the time. We knew we should take steps to move in their direction soon. There was no question in our minds that the best communication of the gospel would take place on a girl-to-girl basis, even as we had seen it work guy-to-guy. But right now we had no girls around to act as leaders. For a while Dean and I had to be both mother and father to a number of the Puerto Rican girls who began to follow their boyfriends to Christ.

The girls from the inner city expose their feelings easily. Several of them went to Colorado and accepted Christ out there. When they came home again, I really started getting it from them. Even in the middle of the night kids would come to me, some of them in tears, and tell me, "This Christ, you can have Him! I don't want to hear anymore from now on. Don't you even breathe a word to me about this Man." They'd even threaten me if I did, because they couldn't see any change in their lives after they hit the streets again.

One girl, whose family was breaking up, came home from Colorado just in time to see her father taken to jail. Gloria's first thought was, "OK, Lord, I'm not going to panic. I know You're here." But almost immediately she came running to me for her help. Her mother wasn't home; her father was in jail. There was just emptiness at home, so she came down to 215 and banged on the door, like a child running to a parent for solutions.

I'd been up very late with the guys and was still sleepy. I had a hard time focusing in on what she was saying. Finally after a long period of listening I saw we weren't moving toward any solution. So I said to her bluntly, "You know something? You walk around here in self-pity and you expect me to give you answers to all your questions."

She was furious and fired back, "You ought to be thankful I can trust you, Bill Milliken! Everybody else has failed me. My family's breaking up is just like having the world pulled out from under me. Don't you understand how that makes me feel about giving myself to anyone, ever again? I can't be torn apart again. Can't you see that?"

I had to tell her, "Look! I'm not God, so I can't answer. I'm sorry I don't know what to tell you to do." I wished I could, but I honestly couldn't. Gloria had accepted Christ, but she had not turned to Him. I had to show her at that moment that I was only human, too. The kids have got to realize this, for they often make us their gods. They turned to us for everything, and physically—not to mention spiritually!—we just couldn't handle it all.

Shortly after this, we acquired our first women helpers. Dean's girl, Sandy, who was in nursing school, and her friend Lyn began to come down to club to help on a volunteer basis. Lyn was so tiny we thought the girls would walk all over her. They both were strong women, though, and the girls soon found out they couldn't put anything over on them. They were all out for their girls, and either of them would have given their right arm, if necessary, to help them. The girls sensed this, but all the same, it was hard at first for them to go to Sandy or Lyn. They still turned to us when they needed someone, because they trusted us. Besides, Dean and I were there all the time, and Sandy and Lyn commuted.

At first the two girls just came to club and introduced themselves, then later they started talking about holding Bible studies.

"That doesn't sound too bad, does it?" one of the girls asked.

"No, it might be good," another said. "What would we talk about?"

"We could talk about being a woman—what God thinks of women—and how important we are," Sandy suggested.

The girls liked that. Being important was a big thing. And the worth of a woman is a curious thing in the city. Sandy had hit home with that suggestion, and the girls' work began. Six or eight girls began to meet together every Thursday, and it was good. The leaders didn't try to pry things out of the group. Instead they cared enough to share themselves—to tell their own experiences, as Christians and before they became Christians. Even their faults they shared openly. This created an atmosphere in which the girls could lean back and be free to say whatever they wanted to say. Soon they decided they needed a girls' apartment, too, and we found a vacancy on Henry Street opposite the rear of 215.

The girls became a family for each other as we had, and began to round out the lives of the fellows in the building behind them, too. On Friday nights the girls would scrape together a meal and invite the guys over for dinner. Part of the fun was the griping and kidding that went on from the time the fellows arrived until there wasn't a crumb left.

"They used to call us over for pizza," one of the guys recalls, "and it would be three inches thick sometimes!" But they didn't leave even a smidgen of tomato paste, you can be sure. Eating was a great thing for us, but the funniest thing about 215 was that you never could find any food around. Every apartment was equipped with a refrigerator and stove, but if you looked in the cupboard you were lucky to find so much as a box of salt. There might be an empty peanut butter jar in the refrigerator, and that was it. (A standing joke among us was that the rats were going on strike because of the lack of food in the apartments.) Food—or rather the search for food—played a big part in our lives, but most of us didn't even know how to light the oven. So Friday night at the girls' place on Henry Street became a thing to look forward to.

One Friday night when I arrived at 215, everyone was standing outside waiting for something to happen. For some reason the girls weren't cooking that night, and nobody knew quite what to do. I had five dollars in my pocket, so I gave it to one of the guys to make the run for whatever he could buy for a fin. Pioneer Market, next door to 215, was used to having us barge in at the last minute before mealtime to buy bananas, milk, cereal, bread or bologna. We scrounged all the dishes we could find in all the apartments, and got along as best we could without the girls that night. On Mondays through Thursdays we could get good, hot, balanced meals at St. Christopher's for a dollar. Then we would sit around and bang on the table, and sing, and laugh and talk with the priests.

Presently, several different Bible study groups got started, and the girls became close in their individual relationships. A new little network of people who care was being woven together on the Lower East Side. Before this the girls had known they were friends, but none of them had dared look for any guarantee as far as trusting each other was concerned. If you told your private business, you knew it would get passed around. Now the girls were learning to trust each other, to feel it when someone else was down—not as a Christian duty, but because they really loved.

Even some of the girls who were making cracks and laughing at their Bible-studying friends got interested. Vickie and her gang had quite a reputation for being the wild drinking crowd among the young girls. We used to sit on a bench with the guys sometimes and hear her crowd whooping and hollering in the park. I began to pray that we could get some girls like that into club. We had the rough guys coming now, but hardly any of the hard core girls had shown up yet.

The first night they walked into club I almost started wishing I hadn't prayed so hard! Vickie walked in with seven of her crowd. They sat down front and stared at me. I was sure they were going to mess up my talk. They sang loudly, and fooled around during the opening part of the meeting, but when I started talking they quieted down along with the other kids and listened. When kids listen with that intensity they just about drain the speaker—sometimes, when I get through, I feel as if my insides have been sucked out.

The night the girls came, I threw out a challenge. "If any of you feels you're close to knowing Christ, or if you really want to make it, we're going to have a camp. And we're going to learn what it means to live for Christ. We're going to come back and walk these streets and mean business. I don't want any phonies. I've got room for thirty, and if you want to come, you can. I don't care if there's only one of you, I'll take you with me all by yourself. But if you don't mean business, don't bother. You can come as a failure. You can come as a miserable person. I don't care about that. What I do want to put the emphasis on is your wanting to make it. If you want to go with Christ, come on up and sign in."

The first person to come to me after the meeting was Vickie. "I wanna go," she said. She is not the type you turn down, so I said, "OK." She came, along with twenty-nine others, and I stuck to what I had said—all my talks were on discipleship. We went back to the city, and I still hadn't had any real talk with her.

Then one night a couple of weeks later I heard a knock at the door. I opened it, and there stood Vickie, bruised and dishevelled, blood trickling from her lip. Her mother had beaten her up, and she had come to me. "Bill, you said if I met Christ things would be different. I asked Christ into my life and nothing happened. Things are worse than ever!"

I didn't even know she had met Christ. But Vickie was in the mood to open up, and needless to say I asked her in. She stood there just inside the door and it all spilled out. Her mother and father were ready to divorce and split up the family. She said that for eight years her father had hardly spoken to her mother. She told me how she wanted to kill her mother—how she had stood over her mother's bed with a knife in her hand at three o'clock that morning, wanting to do her in. "Things are worse than they've ever been," Vickie said, slumping wearily against my door. "You said there's a God. You said Christ loves us. OK, where are They now?"

It was obvious she didn't want to hear platitudes like "Let's open up the Bible and I'll show you something." And I couldn't say, "Let's pray about it." That would have been a nice little escape. So I just sat there and listened, but as I did so, my prayers were going off like a rocket. All the while she was talking, I was jetting them up faster than the blast-offs at Cape Kennedy. And something happened! It was one of those many times when God really gives insight. Instead of babying her, I said, "Why don't you just quit feeling sorry for yourself?"

Here was a girl who had just about every reason in the world to feel sorry for herself. She was only sixteen years old, and so many things had happened to her. But I asked her, "What good is this going to do, feeling sorry for yourself? For the first seventeen years of my life I felt sorry about how miserable I was. And it didn't do anybody any good. If somebody hadn't challenged me, I'd still be sulking in my problems."

She didn't say anything, so I went on, "Maybe I'm just lying to you. Maybe I come here to talk about Christ and to make squares out of all you kids. Maybe I just use this name of Christ. Maybe I've just been using you."

Vickie looked at me steadily with only the faintest spark of interest in her face. I plunged ahead. "On the other hand, maybe Christ is real. And if He *is* real, why don't we make an experiment —a love experiment? You go home, and let's pray daily that you'll learn to love your mother. No matter what she says or does, instead of fighting her, help her. Help her with the dishes, help her with the kids, help her with the work around the house. Maybe your mother won't change right away. But something will happen to you."

She agreed. Her eyes glistened at the thought. We made a pact, and she went home. At first, little things started happening. Vickie reported to me every couple of weeks, "Aw, things are going a little better!" I tried to talk to the mother and father, and absolutely flopped. The mother blamed everything on the father, and the father returned the compliment vociferously.

One morning in February when our world was still fast asleep, the phone rang. You can imagine how I love to be awakened early in the morning, because it's usually well past midnight when I get to bed. I was kind of groggy as I answered, "Who is it?"

"It's Al Jones." Vickie's father—I nearly dropped the phone!

"I just called to tell you I wanna chaperone your trip to Colorado. I hear there might be a possibility of this."

This was February, at 5:30 a.m.! "Al," I said, looking at my watch, "the trip's in July. Why don't we talk about it later?"

"Oh, by the way," Al added casually, "I'm not going to court with the kids. Things are looking a little better. I just wanted you to know. See you later." *BAM!* The receiver clicked, and I rolled over in bed and started to laugh. That was why he'd really called—to tell me something had happened! God was starting to work in the Jones family.

Two weeks later, when Vickie was over, she announced, "You know, I'd like to have a birthday party for my mother. I've never done anything for her. Do you think I could have a surprise party for her?"

I thought this was a great idea but figured the girls should be pulled in at this point. "I'm not too good with this kind of stuff, Vickie. Why don't you go over to Henry Street and plan it with the girls in the apartment. Any money you need, I'll try to get for you."

The very next day she came back, and she was really crying. She looked as if she'd been beaten up. "What happened?" I asked, my heart sinking.

"Well, you told me to go and plan the party with the girls," Vickie said between sobs. "So I did, and I was late getting home. I couldn't tell my mother where I'd been because I want the party to be a surprise. So I got hell!"

My heart was racing 80 miles an hour. I felt sick. Knowing that if it had been myself I'd have said, *To heck with the whole thing,* I asked her, "Do you still want to have the party?"

I was floored—and humbled!—when she replied, "Yes, I really want to have it! I went to bed last night knowing I loved my mother!"

When the time came for the party, we got a friend downstairs to invite Vickie's mother down for a cup of coffee so we could sneak the goodies into their eighth floor apartment. We locked the door and decorated the room quickly. A lot of kids came, and a lot of the mother's own friends, too. When Mrs. Jones came back she knocked on the door before she opened it and flipped on the light. I sensed her embarrassment and anger that we were all dressed up for a party, and here was the guest of honor in her old clothes! My heart sank. Then I watched Mrs. Jones spotting Vickie across the room. The expression in her face changed from night to day.

I wish I'd had a movie camera. The scene that took place at that moment would have won an Academy Award! Those two, just as if there was nobody else in the room, ran and hugged each other. They stood there hugging, tears pouring down their faces. This was it. This was the moment Christ had chosen to bring this relationship together. He was the Key here; the rest of us were fortunate to be the tumblers in the lock.

Vickie's father did chaperone a group of kids to the ranch. He was definitely intrigued. He couldn't understand what had happened to his oldest girl. Vickie had been so rebellious—arrogant, boisterous, defiant at home. Then all at once she seemed to have calmed down and done a complete about-face. When Al asked her what had happened, she told him she had started going to Young Life club. He was so interested that he dropped around at club several times that spring to see for himself what was going on.

When it was time to leave for the ranch in July, we put Al in charge of one busload. There were one hundred and nineteen kids that week, the largest group we have ever taken at one time. With seven children of his own, Al figured he knew how to keep things under control. He stuck a pair of handcuffs in his pocket as he left the apartment.

"You probably wonder why I wanna come so bad," he said to me as we loaded the kids on the buses. "Well, something's really happened to my daughter since she started hanging around Young Life people. I had a feeling maybe I'd find out what happened if I came along with you."

I said, "Al, do me a favor. Just watch what happens this week to kids. Listen. Be alert. And I think you'll find out."

At night on the buses we separated the girls and the guys. Of course, they didn't appreciate this at all, and they tried every possible way to get back together. The boys stayed awake in shifts, trying to outwit the chaperones. Al was doing a good job of staying one jump ahead of them. He was pleased when they called him "Al Private Eye," "Sam Spade," or "I Spy" because he wouldn't let them get away with anything. But sometime during that first night on the bus he dozed off, and when he woke up he found himself handcuffed to the bus! For about ten minutes he panicked as the kids doubled up laughing all around him. Al was their captive till one of the guys produced the key. They had won the first round!

Nobody ever knows what's coming off when a gang of kids leaves New York for Colorado. Most of the guys are right off the street and they haven't been separated from their beer and wine. In addition to the fifths they smuggle aboard, some of them tuck away a box of sneezing powder. At the least expected moment during the trip, everybody on the bus starts to sneeze. Usually somebody brings along a little deal called "Apple Blossom" that creates a terrible stink. And the tricks that get played on guys who go to sleep almost make it worthwhile to stay awake the whole trip!

One fellow dozed off and was snoring noisily with his mouth open when his buddy sneaked up and broke a raw egg into his mouth. The sleeper leaped out of his seat, his knife flashing. "*Who did that?*" Everyone knew he would use that knife as quickly as he'd drawn it, and the snickers all around the bus died quickly. The nearest guys hurried to explain, "Man! We didn't mean anything by it!"

The next day in Chicago there was time for a museum tour before the train pulled out for Colorado. One of the girls was giving Al a real rough time, so right there in front of the Museum of Science and Industry he whipped out the handcuffs. Before the girl knew what was happening, she found herself locked to one of the litter baskets. While the kids teased her, Al took pictures. She made an awful fuss, but it didn't do her any good. After she calmed down, Al unlocked the handcuffs, and everybody knew he had won round two.

Always game, Al opened himself up wide for more trouble when one of the girls came running up to him in the observation car of our train that night. "Where's your handcuffs, Al? Put one on me, please!" Al locked one bracelet on her wrist, and she ran off down the aisle, back to the car where she'd been sitting. When she found this boy she liked and wanted to be with, she locked the other bracelet to his wrist! The guy took a dim view of the whole thing and tried to pick the lock himself. In doing so, they broke the lock. When they came back to the observation car to get Al's help, the guy was steaming. It didn't help much when Al worked the key around and broke it off in the lock!

Just at that moment the conductor came by, and when he saw what had happened he was really shook. He announced he was going to stop the train and call the police. Here we were on an express train with hundreds of other passengers, and he was about to stop the train in order to get two kids separated from each other! "Wait!" Al ordered, as he opened his penknife and finished breaking the lock open. The girl cried. The guy swore at her. The conductor shook his head and muttered, "Crazy kids!" And Al stepped onto the platform between the cars and threw the handcuffs as far as he could into the Nebraska night.

On the last night at the ranch, the whole group always goes up the mountain, and several of the kids tell what it means to them to have Jesus Christ in their lives. The night that Al was there, one of the girls who spoke was Gloria. The loneliness in this girl's life had touched Al before. Her family lived on the next floor up in the Smith Project, and he had seen the family breaking up and dwindling away. The oldest child had gotten married, the mother had gone to live with another man, the father had gone his own way, the son was making it in show business and had his own little world. Gloria, the youngest, was the only one left, and Al had seen how rough life was for her. Now here she was up on this mountain in Colorado telling how she had given her heart to the Lord and how it made such a difference in her life.

As Al listened he thought, "If Gloria can find something new in Jesus Christ to help her, maybe I can, too." While he was still out on the mountain, Al asked the Lord to take over his life and make something of it. Walking back down to the cabin that night, he thought about his fractured home life. Going to court about once a month was almost a family ritual. His wife and he had many problems and were always fighting. The kids were divided; they didn't want to stay in that kind of environment. He could see his family splitting apart at the seams. The courts didn't help, for every trip seemed to aggravate the condition a little more. He had hardly spoken a civil word to his wife in years.

But this night there was hope. Al had seen newness and brightness in the face of a girl in the firelight. He walked into his cabin and found some paper and a pen. Before he had said all he wanted to say, he had filled three pages for his wife back on the Lower East Side. He told her how he was looking forward to coming home and making a real family life for the two of them, instead of the turmoil and fighting they had known for so many years. "I want Christ to enter our home now and run it for us," he wrote. "We can't run it without Him."

When he got home he did put effort into his marriage. He and his wife went together for some marriage counseling, and really made an effort to live a good life for their own sakes and for their children.

Our community within the community was steadily expanding. We were ministering to many problems through feeding, housing, education, athletics, legal assistance. We could use just about anybody who wanted to join us. Doctors, dentists, nurses, teachers, secretaries, preachers, coaches, businessmen—each one was as important as every other. The inner city band wagon was a popular one to be aboard, and we began to have students and drifters, rebels and dreamers, coming by to ask what they could do. Eventually I learned to smile and think, "Just wait and see what happens . . . it's not necessarily what *you* can do for *them*. . . ."

Beyond our own small working unit on the Lower East Side we began to have the makings of a group of professional men from the Wall Street area of Manhattan to help us. They were busy men, the kind who fly to California every week, or over to Asia to put together a business deal, but they were interested in what was happening down here.

One of the first was Curran Tiffany, the man who had come to the apartment with Harv Oostdyk that day when I broke and ran crying to the docks. Curran and I got to having lunch together regularly after that. Somewhere along the line he invited another fellow to join us, and that one invited a friend, and we kept meeting and growing for about two years. Most were older men, and successful, and I felt inferior around them until I saw that they were genuinely interested in being in on something that was affecting people's lives, and in having their own lives affected.

One of the fellows was only a little older than I, and was unmarried too, so we had common ground to talk about our love life. I was very interested in one particular girl just then, and he had a girl too. We fought through a lot of deeply personal things together, just like brothers. Here was a successful businessman, and a guy off the street, yet we had much in common to share deeply.

Girls were important to me personally. I thought they were great, and made no apologies about it. All through my high school and college years I seemed to require the close friendship of a girl as well as the solid friendship of a man. Ever since one night when another guy and I had gone out and very seriously prayed, "Lord, please lead us tonight to the girls You want us to marry," I had been keeping my eyes open for the "right" girl. Now I thought that I had found her, but I was also finding that I had problems within myself which I had not yet resolved.

I remember how guilty I had felt about my thoughts after coming home from Frontier Ranch that first summer after I had made my confession of faith in Christ. Right away, as soon as I got back home, my thoughts were on the girls just as they had been before. When I went to the beach, the girls looked just as good. I hadn't wanted to think the things I was thinking, but still I was doing it. I had felt guilty about it, because in Colorado I'd found something new and wonderful, and already, just a few days later, I thought I'd lost it. I had acquired a conscience, I could tell that, but I didn't seem to have any way of carrying out what my conscience was telling me.

Before Christ took over, it never fazed me when I had thoughts like that about girls. But after I had started in a new direction,

I thought, "Boy! God's going to do me in because I'm thinking this way about that girl!" I hadn't had enough experience with God or Christ or the Bible or anything to know what to do. I didn't have that kind of freedom in His love for me that allowed me to be honest with Him and say, "Well, God, You made me. I'm still Bill Milliken. I may be a new person, but I still have the same thoughts I had before. Help me through them. Thanks for letting me appreciate Your beauty. But don't let me lust after it! I know You don't want me to lust, but I still do it. You'll have to help me change this."

It's easy now, as I look back, to see that the way I showered girls with red roses and long distance phone calls made them feel more important to me than they actually were. I didn't feel at all tied down. I talked a lot and sounded good, but inside I wanted to be free to go my own way. Whenever I found a new girl with whom I could have good conversations or a great time, an old relationship suffered. I was fond of the girls, but some of them were hurt a lot because I wanted to have a good time.

It was just as easy for me to sense moods and needs in a girl friend as it was in the guys on the street. I felt real freedom to talk with them, so they frequently felt comfortable enough to tell me the unusual things they'd never expected to share with anybody. It is not easy to handle this gift of making people feel so special. When someone—especially a girl—commits herself to you by exposing her inner thoughts, it is somewhat shattering for her to discover that other people are equally committed to you, and that you find them *all* very special! I wasn't mature enough to know how to handle this yet, so often I would goof badly, or do something corny, and I could feel the wall go up between us right away.

This was the situation I was in at that time. There was a lovely girl named Jeanie, who also came from Pittsburgh, who could never quite forget her experience at Young Life ranch when she had happily showed my picture to one of her new friends, and two other girls in the same cabin pulled the identical photo out of their own wallets! One of the things that amazes me about those relationships is that the girls knew what I stood for in Christ, and even though I let them down so much, they all seemed to go on in their own commitment to Christ. He was demonstrating that He was a lot bigger than I and my inability to relate.

Jeanie had gone through a period of disliking me intensely because of what she thought I stood for in boy-girl relationships. She questioned whether I would ever be able to commit myself to one girl. She let me know that she felt the trust had been so broken between us that it could never be rebuilt. But although many girls continued to look good to me, and although I often wondered, during my daily encounters in the city, whether God might want me to marry one of the girls I had met there, I found my thoughts kept going back to Jeanie.

Jeanie had softened toward me again by now, and we were growing together slowly through our letters and the times I got back to Pittsburgh for visits. But each time I went back I was a little different type of personality from the time before. This was hard for Jeanie to adjust to. Either I would come home utterly crushed and humbled, or else I would appear very cocky and opinionated to compensate for the dying inside me. I really wanted her to understand how insecure I felt when I was hurting inside and failing. I wanted her understanding so badly that I continually fought with her about it. But she just couldn't understand how badly I was hurting because she was so much a part of suburbia. I was letting out my deepest feelings to her and they didn't make sense in her mind. I tried to avoid the fights by telling her only my successes, but this made me feel dishonest. It gave me a false air of security and over-confidence and she thought I was terribly conceited.

Sometimes when I had gone home to Pittsburgh for a couple of days I would have to scratch out in the car and say, "To hell with this life. To hell with these people. Nobody understands me back here anyhow. They didn't understand me when I was here and they don't understand me now. There's nothing to gain. I'd better just go back to the city and forget her." I'd drive all night back to the ghetto, and then back again to Jeanie to ask, "Can't I communicate? Am I, all my life, going to be unable to really communicate? And if I can communicate, is anybody going to be able to understand what I'm really saying? Or am I so stupid that I just can't say it?"

People back home were still bugging me about finishing college. Nobody could understand, yet I always had this deep feeling in me that my job was to be done *now*. Nobody could understand that Bill Milliken didn't care about being some big shot. Coming from the type of neighborhood, the type of home, the type of church that she did, Jeanie couldn't understand either.

During periods like this we gave up on each other. She went on to college, and periodically I'd call her and tell her I loved her and we would be "on" again for a while. She would decide she didn't want to date at school. Then, other times, she would be absolutely baffled, and would tell me our relationship was over. She would start dating other people, and "fall in love" with someone else. She tried hard; it was a real struggle for us both.

At one point I asked her to marry me, but it was too soon to work out for us. I put the diamond in the safe deposit box, and we gave up with a sense that everything had been done that could be done.

One night after that, I had a date with a very lovely blonde. We went to a dinner party out in Jersey someplace, and the people there were really with it, not the kind of people I usually rebelled against. It was good for me to get out of the city. I didn't tell anyone at the party what I was doing, just said that I was working in New York City. I forgot about the work, or who I was, or what I was trying to communicate. It was a wonderful night, just like old times in a way, so simple and uncomplicated. Later we went to a Marlon Brando movie that was full of adventure. Brando played the kind of loner I looked at and liked—a guy who traveled around. Nobody had him tied down to anything.

That night, and that particular movie, stirred up in me a lot of feelings I'd thought were behind me forever—the same emotions that had driven me to Florida back when I was in college. I recognized them, and they jolted me, because they showed me a facet of Bill Milliken I no longer liked to face!

I was still a wanderer. I didn't like to be tied down. I wanted to have the freedom of knowing I could leave at any time. I did have a responsible job on the Lower East Side, but I could always leave it, in the sense that no great uproar would happen if I did.

As I looked back at my life, I could see that I had always walked out whenever I wanted to. All the time I was driving back through the Holland Tunnel after my date that summer night, I thought of the fun I'd had, of the nice comfortable life so different from the hot streets I was coming back to on the Lower East Side. I got back to the apartment and there were people all over the place, some trying to hustle money from me and others wanting to pour out their problems.

I sat up all night, just thinking, "Man! I'd like to take off. Hit another town. Start something new. Then move on again." I had a vision of myself, going around starting things, then leaving and going on to something else. I didn't like big things. I never wanted to be a part of anything big. But God had taken me up on my commitment and He had been turning our small start at 215 Madison into something very big indeed, far bigger than I had ever bargained for that summer day when I'd gone out into the city streets with that basketball, looking for kids who needed what I had to give.

This was several years later now, and I wasn't that twenty-year-old kid any more. But as I looked around that crowded apartment, and felt the heat, and thought about all the responsibilities I'd taken on one by one, I actually debated throwing some things in the car and just taking off. I didn't know really whether I'd take off for a week, or a month, or forever. I had no ties—except for those kids on the street.

9

Daily Little Dyings

EVERY TIME I felt like punking out, the only thing that kept me were the Eddies, the Bobos, the Clarks, the Rickies, the Glorias, the Vickies, the Taps. It wasn't the neighborhood that kept me. It wasn't the good life. It sure wasn't the adventure, even though that was really what had brought me here. I like adventure, but after the first six months this kind of life isn't adventure; it's hell! It's not enjoyable having problems attack you every time you come home. It's not enjoyable living in the depression and tragedy of people who have been forced to believe they're worthless.

The love God gives me is the only thing that holds me when I want to cut out. By this time people were extremely important in my concept of life and mission. People who have been used, and who have used each other as long as they can remember, need to be loved for their own worth. The one thing that anchors me over and over again is this thought: Outsiders have done this to the people of the city all their lives—come and gone. Someone comes into the neighborhood and stays long enough to write a research paper, do a thesis, put together a book, and then he moves out to a better job, a higher degree, a greater position. It happens all the time. Outsiders use the people, pull out, and step up, without realizing the effect on those left behind. So much of my thinking about the people, about the work, about myself was shaped during the weak moments such as that night when I was so close to leaving the Lower East Side.

The guys here have been beaten so long. They are told they're bad almost from the moment they can hear. Many of them naturally come to think of themselves as inferior. Look with me at a mother with three children. She began to bear children at fourteen. The father has left home. She is so burdened with unfulfilled needs that she vents her own frustrations on the children. They're close to her twenty-four hours a day, so they get it all the time as she screams at them for one thing after another. What does it do to a three-year-old to be told he's going to get cut to pieces as soon as the company leaves? And what happens to him when he slips his hand into his mother's as she talks to a friend, and her only response is a slap? What happens when he starts at three years of age to talk about how he's going to be a junkie, when he can name the whiskey he wants to get high on and talks about how nice he felt? These little kids miss out on so much of life from the very beginning, and they grow up feeling they're not worth much.

The whole idea of little kids playing in the street is shocking, if all your life you've played in the big, green, grassy park or on your own private manicured lawn. The junkies hanging out on almost every corner shock you if you've never known anyone who even smoked "pot." The girls having babies without being married shake you up when you've been oriented to a society that makes a girl an outcast who becomes pregnant outside marriage. Waking up in the middle of the night, hearing people scream at each other in the next apartment, makes you shudder if you've come from a neighborhood where no one raises his voice, or they live too far away to hear them. Even the fact that people stay up till 4:00 a.m. and then sleep till afternoon is unsettling. All of these things are hard to accept, yet all of them happen over and over to reinforce your cultural shock. Little by little you begin to lose the idea that you are in the city to help somebody else. You lose it because you need help so badly yourself.

The new people all come along somewhat the same route I stumbled over. You get to the place where you hate the city and you have no idea how anyone can ever help it, least of all yourself. And since that was your reason for coming in the first place, you are overwhelmed by the fact that first of all you have to learn. You have to learn why the situation is as it is. You have to learn about the people. About the culture. About the environment. And you have so much to learn that you don't have time to think about helping anybody else. You have to get your bearings because you have truly lost your equilibrium. And before you can make any sort of contribution to others, you first have to regain a balance within yourself.

To do that, you start by going around, absorbing whatever you can through whatever contacts you have made. You stand and watch. You sit at the counter, or on the park bench, in the subway, on the stoop. You smile, or say a word. And you swallow hard and absorb the "Get lost!" or the kid running away when you walk up. And you absorb the leer and the rude pass, if you're a girl.

But you also absorb the "Good morning!" and the neighbor who holds the door open in the project when you're loaded down with laundry. And the little hands that reach up to yours. And the French fries the young kid sticks in your face with a big grin—"You're hungry, ain't you?" You find out early that you are here, not at all to help according to your own notions, but to absorb and to respond and to learn what you can. You become aware that the whole matter of giving has to come spontaneously rather than in a planned kind of way. You give because the situation arises, not because you say, "Well, here I am. I've come to give to you." You find yourself listening to somebody's problem, then telling yours to him, when you never intended doing that at all. You begin to develop the art of listening to what people are *really saying* instead of what you want to hear being said! And you find yourself learning about receiving, through simple, simple things. You begin to see that by denying people the opportunity to give, you really hurt them. It depreciates a person when you can't receive from him, because in a sense you reject the one sure thing he has to offer—his freedom to give.

We measure things so unconsciously by money. It takes quite a while for most of us to learn how to let city people give to us. Somebody offers to go buy us a hot dog, and our conditioned reaction is, "No, thank you." In reality, they very much want to spend their quarter on that hot dog. We're thinking, "I'm sure that's their last quarter," but we learn to say, "That sounds great.

Thanks. I'd love it." In ways like this you learn to receive, and in emotional ways, too.

The first summer you spend in the city you think, "I'm so fortunate! I've had a solid family background. I've got a lot of friends. I'm equipped with a lot of emotional strength. I can really give emotionally to these people." Then all of a sudden, there you are in an unfamiliar situation which takes away a lot of your solidarity, and a lot of your security. And you're vulnerable. This is very necessary, because only as you become vulnerable can you accept what people have to give. It is amazing how much you are given—because you really know so little. You find yourself in the position of receiving, and the "poor people" in turn are in the position of being able to give emotionally to you because you are needier than they!

The uninhibited spirit of the ghetto person has negative aspects as well. A person who is lacking in controls will behave irresponsibly. City kids act on impulse much more readily than those who are raised in a more structured society. In a disciplined environment we are constantly told what is right and what is wrong, so that we develop, sometimes too rigidly, controls on our impulses. In the city you don't find this; people respond to what they feel. This is one of the reasons so much trouble occurs in the city. If a kid feels like stealing, he steals. That's his impulse, and there is nothing pressing down on that impulse to restrain him. He will be honest in telling you he loves you, which is beautiful. But he will be just as honest in telling you he wants to cut so-and-so's throat, which isn't beautiful at all.

As we live here on the Lower East Side, we provide an image of someone who has at least some inner controls. Through our relationships we can somehow communicate the idea that controls are valuable, and that they can lead to praiseworthy, responsible behavior. We who come from the outside do have some beautiful values to bring into the ghetto from middle-class suburbia. Once we get our balance, it is our responsibility to relate these.

Those who have grown up without restraints also have things which are tremendously significant for us to learn, a freedom which we desperately need to feel and to express. On the other hand, we are equipped to be the corrective agent in less desirable behavior. We can demonstrate consistency and self-discipline. The whole idea of a girl saying she is going to baby-sit, for example, and then being disciplined enough actually to follow through on the promise, is foreign. That girl needs elementary help in simply getting up off her behind, taking her feet and setting them on the floor and moving them towards the door of the place where she is supposed to baby-sit.

This is a new kind of behavior for many city kids. Little things, such as going to school on time, have become a natural part of the whole middle-class self; we don't even think about not doing them. They have become spontaneous reactions, rather than actions we have to force upon ourselves. Just simple little things, such as going to school in the morning, or being at a meeting on time, seem impossible for many of the kids to grab hold of.

These impossible things build up inside people until they are ready to burst. This is a partial explanation of why there is more violence in the ghetto. So you listen, and you sympathize, and you put your arm around them and say, "I care about you." But there is a point too at which you can't just let them stew in their own juice any more. You confront them and say, "OK, we can't do anything about the past. It was lousy. It's lousy what the white man has done. It's lousy what your parents have done. It's lousy what your relationships with people have done. It's lousy what's happened to you. *But what are you going to do about it?* Let's start with today. What moves are you going to make today? Where are you going?"

At this point my friend Duke used to get mad at me and yell, "All right, I'm going to do this now!"

Then I could hold him to it. If he didn't follow through, I could come back at him with, "Why didn't you do it? *You* said you were going to. It wasn't my idea." You have to be careful about getting a guy mad; it takes a long time in a relationship before this can be done in love. It's usually when guys argue with me that I get rough with them. When a guy is really down, hurting and dying inside, that's not the time to kick him. You put your arm around him and say, "Come on. Let's pray about it. Get it out of your system. I don't have the answer for you, but let's ask God together."

We know so little how these guys feel. They see so many people being damaged, people who grew up in the same environment they're in, the same kind of home situation. They see people they know going on dope, strung out, prostituting to get money. And they can't see how there's any possibility of being any different themselves; they assume the same things will happen to them, too. This kind of thing probably bothers more kids than we know; the fact that they see so many people failing all the time makes them sure they won't be exempt. It almost creates a defeat. It makes them vulnerable to taking junk, or drinking, or being a prostitute, or having a breakdown. We have to look for the strong place in a kid and build on it. We have to point out where the differences lie, the positive relationships, the love, the things that are going in his favor. And we have to work towards convincing him that he *can* think constructively about his own life. We need to *affirm* him!

Every day in the city has its ups and downs. Sometimes you have an unusually good day. Sometimes you have an unusually bad day. But most of the days are made of ups and downs. I'm a guy who is emotional, and who has finally become free enough to express it instead of keeping it bottled up inside. Being this kind of person brings both gifts and problems with it. Along with the ability to express oneself often comes the tendency to fall apart.

Some of the guys who come to us can't even smile or laugh appropriately. When a person's sense of humor is erratically off, it's very often an indication that his whole situation is pretty off-balance. And it's tough, when you really care about the person, to see how bad things are.

One guy who lived in our apartment had a completely inappropriate sense of humor. None of his friends understood him. He won admiration by his burglaries, and the only way he knew how to make human contact was by spending his stolen money lavishly on others. He would give a guy $50 to blow on a good time. And when he wanted to get through to a girl friend, he would grab her by the hand and pull her around like a child would pull a toy. This was his only means of reacting. One time Dean went to visit this young man in a prison. Nobody had been there to see him in three months. When Dean walked in, the boy just looked at him blankly and said, "You got a dime? I want to get a candy bar." There was no human recognition. This fellow was completely unable to relate emotionally to anyone.

I don't think any of this would bother us so deeply if we hadn't come to love people so much that we want what's right for them. That's why we react. That's why we hurt. That's why we die a little. When one of the boys in our apartment gets his girl pregnant and calls at three in the morning to say they're running away, we hurt. When we hear that a friend who's fourth in his class at Prep School hasn't shown up for two weeks, we hurt. When we watch an intelligent girl turn in blank papers at school because she's so worried about her Lesbian partner in the hospital, we feel the sickness in our own stomachs. We hurt because it's so wasteful. Sometimes we get the feeling that we have to back off just to protect ourselves. The more you get to know a kid, the more you care; and the more you care, the more it hurts inside.

I think back to one night when I came in off the streets at two in the morning to find a note on my door. Richie had been shot accidentally, just above the heart, and he was dying. Richie was a halfback on our football team and he had made something like fourteen touchdowns that season by means of a favorite trap play that went around Snake, our guard. Snake could always open up the way for Richie, and they had been looking forward to the upcoming championship game. Richie had so much going for him—he had met the Lord; he had parents who cared about him; he had started night college. He had really been making progress. All the while I was driving to the hospital I kept asking, "God, why? Why Richie?"

When I walked into the hospital I found the situation tense and sad. There were the mother and father, whom I knew fairly well, sunk in grief. There was Snake, who had run interference for Richie so many times. There was the kid who had accidentally shot Richie as he was showing off a gun. He had been a little high at the time, and Richie had just said, "Don't fool around with it," when the gun went off, catching Richie in the lung about a quarter of an inch above the heart. The father, crying softly, told me the doctors gave Richie about a twenty percent chance of living beyond the emergency operation which was now in progress. I recall the doctor coming down to ask for a couple of men to give blood to replace what they were using from the blood bank.

Snake and I asked if we could go up. Neither of us had ever given blood before. They put us in the same room at the same time. Our heads were real close; I couldn't see the blood coming out of myself, but I could see it coming out of Snake's black arm. I lay there thinking that here was Snake opening up another way for Richie to make it, to go, to be alive. And here was I, too; Snake was black and I was white, and that didn't matter at all, the blood from both of us came out red. I was thinking about Christ's blood being spilled for all men, and how because of Him we could live life fully, together, one body, no matter where we grew up. Now our blood being given for Richie could bring life to him, and we were made one, in a new way, by this experience.

When I saw Richie the next day he had tubes into his heart, his nose, his feet—all over the place. He was a mess, and no one thought he would ever play football again. But he did. And the night we gave him the "Most Valuable Player Award" at our football banquet he stood before 450 of his teammates, friends and neighbors and said, "You know, at one time this would have really made me feel great; but the fact that I know Christ is what's important. My biggest thrill is that He let me live."

All of us together were learning how to "stand by the door," as Sam Shoemaker so aptly put it. We had learned we couldn't make it by ourselves, locked away in our ivory towers, and we would never be able to hear others knocking on the door either if we were way back inside where it was warm and quiet and comfortable. Right by the door—in the draft and cold from the outside—we could sometimes take hold of a groping hand and pull somebody inside. We knew we couldn't merely call on our own resources any more. In order to succeed we were forced over and over again into a dependence on God and on each other; and we were well aware that if we didn't have that dependence and that desire to be dependent, we weren't going to make it.

A seventeen-year-old mother comes and tells me she's getting married in a month. This is the case with so many kids, not just in the ghetto either. It frightens me to think of the difficulties she will have. Just being in the adolescent stage makes it impossible for her to know much about relationships. And she will get married with all kinds of strikes against her just because of that lack of real relating between herself and her boy friend. One person strikes out; the other strikes back; they have nothing going between them but this repercussion. This happens because of the impulses, the lack of inner control. Many street kids have never observed healthy relationships among parents, friends, brothers and sisters. So what can they base a marriage on? They don't understand commitment.

This is another way in which our growing community must help. Even in our relations with other staff members we need to communicate something of the idea of our commitment. The kids have to be able to see this, so they can draw a frame of reference from it. We want so badly for these kids to understand something of relationship, of commitment. We want our relationships with them to give support even when we can't be around. But it doesn't always come out happily in the end.

I was driving down Madison Street in the car one afternoon when a guy called out, as they often do. I stopped. Apache wanted to hustle a quarter from me. Since I knew he drank a lot, I said, "No. You're just hustling me and I don't go for that."

There was a pause, because he knew he wouldn't get the money. Then suddenly he said, "I'm lost, man. I really feel lost. You gotta talk to me. I'm lost. Lost."

"Well, let's talk. I don't have to go where I'm going."

But Apache said, "No, go ahead. I promised somebody I'd meet him. Give me forty-five minutes and come back."

I told him, "OK. I'll get out of what I was going to do and I'll be back here in forty-five minutes. Sure you don't want to talk now?"

"No, I gotta meet this guy. I'm late now."

"All right. I'll be back." I drove off and canceled out the meeting I was supposed to have at 5 o'clock, and got back to 215 Madison a little before the time was up. Apache wasn't there. Nobody'd seen him since he ran over to the car. All they knew was that he'd gone to meet somebody. I waited a while and then drove around trying to find him, but he wasn't anywhere. Finally I gave up and said to one of the guys on the street, "Here's my phone number. Have him call me."

The next morning early I went out and the guys told me Apache was dead. I felt like hell inside—another life wasted! He had died shortly after he had left me to meet his friend. An overdose of narcotics. It was a sick death, a matter-of-fact death. Everyone knew Apache, hung out on the same steps with him; hardly anybody went to the funeral. He was lost and everybody knew it. He had been meeting death for the past six months, and people wanted to duck the memory as soon as possible. They had seen death watching him from the other side of the fence.

10

Gold in the Mire

SOMETIMES you look around and ask, "What's the problem? Are there just too many people together?" The standard answer is that it's the environment. But what makes up the environment? Everybody blames the problem on the other person. Once in a while you end up thinking there are evil demons all over. And then it happens—the explosion. All the things that have built up inside of you come pouring out. All of a sudden you're crying out how you hate the city, how you despise the ugliness, the impulses, the weakness, the tragedies. You hate that power structure and system that has forced and allowed ghettos to happen and to remain. Some days you lose perspective entirely and feel it's all hopeless, and you ask yourself, "What am I doing here?" You lose sight of the fact that here's where God wants you to be, whether anything happens or not. You're called to Him, and He wants you where He wants you whether the day is good or bad.

At other times you're on top of everything. "Man! This is great! We're going to make it!" Or you hear yourself exclaiming, "Hot dog!" and you laugh because you feel you can do anything. Christ gives His disciples the security of victory. He changes people, gets them together, and gets them going. We need a strong group within the ghetto who can taste victory and strength even in the midst of defeat. A group of people who can dance the dance of life in the midst of a great struggle! But the group has to realize always that the problems will never be totally defeated.

One of the problems we are grappling with now is the whole matter of education—the kind of education that's really relevant to guys in the street. Schools try to give slum kids the same kind of education that's given to kids in the suburbs—even the standardized tests have been geared to children with that background until recently—and it just doesn't work. So teachers think the kids are dumb, and they communicate that feeling to the kids, and you wind up with that old stumbling-block of guys growing up assuming that they're not worth much.

To a certain extent I understand how that happens, because people thought I had a real low IQ, and so I thought so, too. "Look out for this guy Milliken," they would say. "He knows how to get to people, but that's it." Then I took some tests that showed my IQ was even a little above average; the problem lay in my mental blocks, inferiority problems, not in lack of ability. The same thing happens to these kids. They're told they're inferior for so long that they believe it, when in reality they've missed out on some of the important mechanics of living. With me it was the mechanics of reading that was poor, so people thought I was dumb; *I* thought I was dumb; I got so I just didn't care, so I did poorly on tests and was stuck with the results.

I never read a textbook in college, I just spot-read. All my learning was situational. This is how kids in the ghetto learn. The street kid doesn't read books, but he knows so much. He knows what's happening. I never took notes in class, but I could always remember what a professor had said. That's the way the kids pick up knowledge in the streets. They haven't got the mechanics, but they have deep insights. They have an education that many suburban kids never get or will get in a lifetime.

Clark was a perfect example of how really sharp guys can get lost in the shuffle of the city schools. Before his week at the Young Life ranch, he hadn't seen any real purpose in life—he didn't really know what he was going to do, or how he would go about doing it. In ninth grade he was directed into a vocational high school. He figured it was too late now to change to an academic high school, and he had lost interest in the vocation. He was, in a sense, resigned to making the best of a mediocre situation, and prepared to settle for any job he could get after graduation. In the ghetto, this sort of educational misdirection is all too typical, and it leads to the dead-end situations, lack of sense of personal worth, and "What's the use?" attitudes with which we were becoming so familiar.

We began to see that sending our boys and girls into a routine academic situation was like tossing them to the wolves. So many of the mechanics of learning were missing. Clark felt so inferior in high school that he hardly even made it through trade school. Eddie flunked every subject. It wasn't till they both moved into the apartment, and the two of them began challenging each other, that they picked up skill and motivation in learning. We made arrangements with a private school in Newark, New Jersey to take some of our fellows. Every morning they tore out of 215 in our Econoline bus. At his city high school Eddie used to be late every day and nobody ever said anything; in fact, if he showed up at class three times a week, that was good. But at Newark Prep it wasn't as easy to miss school. This was a new kind of pressure. The prep-school teachers insisted on a certain level of behavior. When the fellows were late, the disciplinarian called them in and said, "Look, men, I don't know what your problem is. I don't want to hear you had a flat tire, or you didn't have money to pay the toll through the tunnel. These are all things you have to take into consideration yourselves. You be here, and you be on time."

The teachers also expected students to study. They piled on homework; it was good for the guys, but it was hard. These were new values that were not a part of the street culture. "You gotta be on time . . . you can't be absent . . . you can't be getting C's, you gotta get A's or B's." These were pressures that some of the fellows could withstand, but others began to buckle under them. They began to arrive even later. They began to be absent even more. They failed and failed and failed again, even though they had plenty of college potential.

One of the greatest problems in growing up in the city is simply learning how to become worthwhile. Self-respect is probably the strongest single factor in succeeding. Duke, for instance, wanted very much to be a number-one individual. He wanted everyone to take notice and say, "There goes Duke. He's a smart guy." One of the things that hurt the most was his knowledge that he had a lot inside of him which just wouldn't come out. The one word he hated most to hear was *potential,* because it made him feel so helpless. People would tell him, "Duke, you've got so much potential!" But he didn't know where to turn. So many things fascinated him; his mind would go in fifty directions, and he was dragged down by his inability to concentrate on any one thing. As a result he just gave up.

Duke told me that the people who were most helpful to him in his growing-up years had two things in common: "They were able to key me up about life, and they could key me up about myself."

Education was becoming an important thrust in the city. It began to compete with the image of the gang . . . the wino . . . the junkie. When Bobo and Eddie were just kids, there was no such thing as thinking of college; college was something like the stars. No one thought of trying to make it that far, for it was all anybody could do to stick it out through high school. At this point, however, a good image was shaping up for education. There was a growing recognition among the young blacks that education was the key to success, that knowledge was power.

As we saw the importance of our role in their education, we started sponsoring a few fellows in prep school. This cost us $1,000 per year apiece. We knew the budget would be wiped out in no time at that cost. We kept dreaming and praying toward some kind of educational step we could take right in the city that would help more guys and girls gain an appreciation of their own value. It was thrilling to watch kids respond to the love of the Saviour, and then to observe the hunger in them to be somebody.

The idea of a transitional step in education came to us as we worked with Harv Oostdyk and his staff in the Harlem area. We could see the need for a glorified tutoring situation, perhaps at several levels. In this way we could lead kids personally, at their own speed, from the impressive sum of human knowledge they had already acquired just by living, and add to it the more technical and formal areas of learning.

Even the language used in the public schools was foreign to the street-oriented kids, so they had grown accustomed to tuning out even if they didn't drop out. We began to understand that "rap" was necessary to learning. Rap is the language that people with a street orientation use when they talk seriously. It has a peculiar grammar, a peculiar rhythm, a peculiar vocabulary all its own. It is somewhat the baring of one's soul, the getting down to the raw guts of life from the perspective of the street. On the other hand, rap was not used at all on College Entrance Exams, and some of the guys were looking to us to get them into college.

The first step was merely an exposure to a larger, more disciplined world. We took a group of fellows to Washington, where they watched Congress in session, and met some of the senators and congressmen. They caught a vision of where they might be able to go and what they could do. Other trips to Philadelphia and Boston further bridged the gap between the ghetto and the principles of democracy. Anybody who was completely fouled up educationally was welcome in this program. It was a sort of factory for motivation, a way of exposing people to education and the possibilities of it, a way of moving them from self-centeredness and self-concepts into enlarged concepts of an expanding world that became increasingly *their* world. The difference between the young people of the city, and the ones I had grown up with in suburbia, I discovered, was not a matter of intelligence but of background. Harv Oostdyk gave consultation on how we could improvise a flexible curriculum to link the academic situation with the world of the street.

The main breakdown in education seems to occur because of the separation between these two parts of a city kid's life. Academic study seems totally meaningless to the person in the streets. We dug for ideas which would gear a curriculum to the familiar life of the city. We sought out material to use in sociology and history classes, and came up with some contemporary writings from the city. *The Autobiography of Malcolm X,* for instance, fascinated the poorest reader because it spoke of struggles and places and issues that were familiar. If we could show why Malcolm X developed his political power, then we might begin to study political power in general. We could see that education would need to relate clearly to the social community our kids recognized, so they could begin making academic generalizations out of their own experiences in the street.

The kids I know are great at making generalizations. Their intuitive powers and sensitivity to life's problems are better than those of their middle-class counterparts. Their ability to persist in a logical series, their skill in handling English grammar, their knowledge of historical facts all are weak. These are things they need help with before they can move up in school, or on to college. We tried to show the guys as we worked that they already had a lot of informal education, but that in school they could learn to relate what they did know to areas they had never understood.

No matter what field a person is fitted to enter he is always working from the place where he stands. You can't get away from that. We reasoned that if we could get these kids excited about the relationship between themselves and their community, between that community and the whole country, between the United States and the rest of the world, this could provide the links between the world they know and the wider worlds of academic education.

Two things we felt strongly—one, that education and street life were *not* two different things; two, that whatever a person is doing on the street can be improved by further education. These two pegs were the cornerstones on which we began to build our program of on-the-street education.

11

Helping Each Other

When we take our guys out to the suburbs to speak in a church, the apprehension or fear about having inner city people in their all-white congregations turns out to be unfounded. The most brilliant members are often moved to tears by the qualities within these fellows. They begin to see how Christ can unleash the resources of leadership. And this bears witness not only to Jesus Christ, but also to the potential that lies in the ghetto waiting to be tapped. As one of our most faithful committeemen says, "When you take the candor of their inner city culture and bring Jesus Christ into it, you have a great resource for the nation and the world, as well as for their own neighborhood!"

Bobo was scared to death when I approached him one day and said, "Bobo, we have a younger group of Christians now, and I want you to start a Bible study with them." He didn't feel at all comfortable about stepping out into this new position, but he decided, "I might as well start now if I'm gonna start." There were really sharp guys in that crowd and they were attracted to Bobo's leadership.

This step into the Bible study showed Bobo what Christ was doing for him. Other evidences followed as he went to the ranch as a junior counselor. Then he came onto the staff, first part-time and then full-time. Eventually we put him in charge of fourteen fellows living in the apartments at 215.

Bobo's ability to lead was not new, of course. He had always wanted to lead, he had always been interested in younger kids. He loved them and wanted to mean something to them. The only image he had been shown by the older fellows as he grew up himself was the gang-fighting image. Now he was determined not to lead younger guys coming up under him into being tough guys. Now he could point them in a new direction. It was great to see Bobo leading club for the younger brothers of the guys he used to fight!

One day I got a call from Bellevue Hospital. They had a young fellow, sixteen years old, who had been under psychiatric care and whom they wanted to release into some constructive situation other than his own family. I told them we could take him into our apartments; then I got hold of Bobo. "You've got a new kid down in 215. You'd better go take a look at him."

Mike was a quiet young man, tall as a beanpole, who looked more like twenty than sixteen. Bobo got him settled into the apartment, and things went smoothly until one day he noticed a broken window. The guys all said that Mike had broken it, so Bobo told him he would have to pay for a new window. When Mike said, "No," Bobo explained that he would have to shoulder his own responsibility in the apartment or else he would have to leave. Mike didn't like that so he went to the closet and came back with a hatchet and a knife.

Bo was shook, but he got Mike to sit down and talk. As they discussed the problem, Mike's attitude and voice tone quieted down. Bobo told Mike about his own struggle with temper, and how he had defended himself all his life by fighting. Then he told Mike how he was changing gradually since he had turned his life over to Christ. He let Mike know that he wanted to be his friend, that he was really concerned about what was happening to him. But he also put it plainly to Mike that he was on his own, and would have to become a man even if he was still only sixteen.

Two weeks later Bo was in his room reading his New Testament when Mike pushed the door open and said, "Hey! Guess what? I became a Christian two weeks ago!" We began to see a gradual change taking place. But the real confirmation came several months later, when the social worker assigned to Mike took him back to the doctor at Bellevue for tests. The report was a complete OK!

Every morning Bobo sets the alarm for 6:30 so he can wake Mike up and get him started to school on time. Like a mother, he props Mike up on the edge of the bed and asks, "Mike, are you awake?" Then he falls back into his own bed till 8:00 when the other fellows need to get up. A few minutes later, if Bobo doesn't hear anything, he gets up again, frequently to find Mike fast asleep. At this point Bobo differs from standard maternal procedure—he goes to the refrigerator, takes out a big bottle of ice water, and dumps it all over Mike. This treatment will usually cure oversleeping for a long time to come! Mike usually gets up and out on time, but last night he stayed up too late watching TV—so today Bo moved the TV into his own room so he can control the use of it. The problems Bobo faces are those of any household, multiplied by fourteen male adolescents! There are money problems, personal problems, housekeeping problems—getting the guys to change their sheets, replace worn-out light bulbs and wash their socks, checking on how they feel about school, about work, about club, about themselves.

Mike is not outstanding, but he's making it. We see Mike's father on the street and he tells us how much he respects Bobo, and how thankful Mike's mother is for the way we took Mike in when he needed help they couldn't give him. "But it hurts a lot," he adds, "because Mike loves Bobo better than he does us."

Mike still hates the "drunk" image his father portrays, but through the gift of love which he finds in Bobo and the other fellows in the apartment, he is gaining a new love for his mother and father.

"It's the *people* who make the apartment," one boy told a visitor. "We share clothes, food, money, everything. If there's a problem, we all talk about it, pray about it. Together we manage. The guys are their own parents—we take care of each other. It doesn't matter about the hot water being all gone, or about the cockroaches, or about the cupboard being bare, because we've got something more important than that. No matter how rich you are, you can't buy the relationships we have at 215."

Heading up the apartments demands a lot of a man—in time, patience, understanding, courage. Always there are problems staring you in the face. Always you are bounced off balance by failure. One of the hardest things for us to do is just to give up on a guy. It's not easy to discipline big guys, eighteen or nineteen years old. In some cases, you counsel and counsel. You love and love, and a guy still doesn't try to live up to the standards, doesn't try to follow any advice. Then all you can do is tell him, "Maybe this isn't the place for you to find yourself."

We don't always have the answer. This, in itself, is part of the answer—the fact that there is no pat solution. We have to back off to a point where we don't know, and just put the problem up to Christ. If there *is* an answer, He has it. Learning this has been so great. It takes so much pressure off when you know you can leave things up to Him. We're not trying to build an empire; we're not competing for stars in a crown; we're not keeping scores with God. Our job is just to be present, to work as hard as we can, and to let Him take care of the results. This does away with the strings we so easily attach to love; it means we can love for love's sake. If a person refuses Christ, we can still love him. We serve him; we give him the education and the home; we point him toward Christ, and let him choose. But we don't have to compel him into our frame of mind, we don't have to force him into our mold.

At Young Life staff conference in Colorado we began to see further evidence that the inner city people had valuable gifts for people anyplace. Bobo and I ended up in the same Bible study group together, and I was afraid he would clam up. A few years ago he would have done so, thinking the Young Life guys from suburban clubs were so brainy and had such great theological backgrounds. Many of those middle-class fellows do have the ability to intellectualize, and they have a firm knowledge of the content of the Bible. But I was proud of Bobo. He was willing to enter into the study with his own special gifts. He could zero in on the meaning of a passage and relate it to the brass tacks of life. He had the knack of making a truth specific and practical. While those men who could intellectualize were feeding Bobo with content, he was feeding their suburban minds with his city heart.

From our first summer in New York, our pattern has been to transport kids out of the city streets and into the totally different atmosphere of the Colorado ranches. We developed the knack of spotting a guy who was ripe for the experience and zeroing in on him. That was what we did when I decided we should break into a new area which we called "the hill." I'd been hanging around the park in that area and I couldn't help but notice Ollie, who was tall and lanky and had such a big mouth. Kids didn't hate him, but he bugged them because he had such an ability to use his mouth, usually in the wrong way. Something about Ollie commanded attention. Even though he was negative in a lot of ways, he could express himself very well for such a young kid. I saw this ability and thought how terrific it would be if his gift were channeled properly. So I got him to go to the ranch.

I guess I'll have to admit that I regretted it a number of times before the trip was over. I put Ollie in my cabin, and his big mouth got on my nerves. After a few days I tried to have some quiet, serious times in the cabin at night. Some of the guys were really interested by this time, but Ollie kept ruining everything with that big mouth. We'd be getting to an important thought and Ollie would crack some filthy joke or take the Lord's name in vain, and throw the guys' minds completely off what we had been saying.

One evening as we were leaving the dining hall, I'd had it. Ollie had been mouthing off in the dining room, so I pulled him over to a big rock and we sat down together. I learned something about Ollie that night: Whenever I say to him, on a one-to-one basis, "I just want to talk to you," he knows I mean business and sobers up quickly. I started by telling him off, and at first he mouthed back at me sharply. But I kept hitting one point from several different angles—his mouth, and the corruption that came out of it, and how this was ruining the week for some of the other guys in the cabin. "I don't care whether you believe in Christ or not, you can at least give the other guy a chance. . . . I *do* care, Ollie. Inside, I really do care about you. I wouldn't be out here arguing with you if I didn't care." People need to know we love them. Telling someone you love him, man-to-man, isn't wishy-washy at all if you express it in a manly way.

Ollie saw I meant it, and he started to listen. Then right there on that rock, with guys walking past and calling out to us, he bowed his head and prayed out loud that Christ would take over his life and make him different. When we got back to the cabin everybody noticed the biggest difference—not in what he said to the gang, but in what he didn't say.

God works so differently in different people. Sometimes it's shown in a quiet guy's being able to say something. But with a loud-mouthed guy, it's the silence that speaks. The minute Ollie stepped inside the cabin he shut his mouth. Every night after that he lay there reading the Bible; he didn't enter into the discussion with one word. This spoke to the guys more profoundly than anything he could have expressed.

Clark had his own unique gifts to give. Here was a guy who was nothing in the gang structure, yet who slowly emerged as the backbone of all our early work. Boot, Bobo, Eddie—any of those early guys can think back and see that Clark was the most consistent guy in the whole work. They all looked up to him. Clark couldn't believe he was that important, which was good for him. One thing I deeply respected was the way he stood up to me, once he started getting the vision. He has always loved me enough to come to me and tell me where I am wrong. He wouldn't sound off or criticize; he would just come and say, "Bill, I'd like to talk to you." Just as I do with the kids. He would really pour himself out to me when he thought I was rubbing somebody wrong, or was going in a wrong direction. Another strong characteristic was Clark's ability to see my point of view. He could really listen to me and not just try to get his own point across. He was the quiet one, but so much the key one too. The Andrew of the Lower East Side.

They don't all make it, though. For every Ollie there's a Gary who walks out and goes back to bumming and getting high. For every Bobo there's a Larry who has the gifts but doesn't want to put out what it takes to develop them. For every Clark there's an Apache who can't see beyond the next needle full of junk.

12

Lives in Young Life

THAT GROUP of professional men whom God gave me often counteracted the daily dyings which made me lose sight of victory. First, we were praying together. Then they started giving money towards different projects. I began to introduce them to kids, and they brought friends to club meetings. Eventually I told them about the concept of a Young Life Committee, and explained that they were already doing the things for me that Young Life Committees were doing all over the country for other staff men and women. They were already involved naturally on the Lower East Side, without knowing how well they fitted into the organizational structure. I invited them to keep on doing what they had been doing over the past months, only now with the understanding that they would be my official committee. They agreed because they were already a part of the work with me.

What I appreciate most about the Committee is that it formed out of our common need to know more about Christ; we first met for that purpose. Later, when the group evolved into an official Committee, it still focused on Christ, yet its vision reached into the neighborhood. We had already gone through the baby stage and the adolescent stage; now, as we became a Committee, we entered adulthood as a group. We knew each other. We had prayed for each other. We had hurt together, gone through crises together.

Often a group of persons gets pulled together as a planning group or a committee before the individuals have ever gotten to know each other. This is like being forced into adult responsibilities before they have matured through the childhood and adolescent stages. They don't know each other, so they come up with methods that are unsuited to that particular group. And the project lacks life because they're trying to come up with better methods before they themselves are striving to become better men. Their emphasis is on what they are doing out there, rather than on what Christ is doing inside.

With the bankers, stockbrokers, lawyers and others who became the Young Life Committee, it was different. God was molding us together. Each man brought different gifts. Some possessed the gift of asking hard questions—a lawyer deals with hard situations all the time. I needed the kind of discipline those questions provided. For example, the Committee didn't realize the financial status of our work. That was my fault. I was proud. I didn't know how to receive. But God was starting to teach me this by breaking down my pride.

At the time when the Committee became official, our staff had been scraping, really scraping, to make ends meet. We had our electricity turned off many times. Once we started paying our own rents, after the church quit paying for the apartment, we almost got thrown out any number of times. The Committee started off by putting up about one-third of my salary. Then they raised it to half. Eventually they committed themselves to paying my full salary every month. This meant committing themselves to raising the money or else putting it up out of their own pockets.

The Committee became involved in far more than financial matters. One year each Committeeman took a particular fellow to be responsible for. I told the Committeeman, "Now I expect you to help this kid." I also told each kid, "Hey! I want you to really get this guy on the ball." Each of them went out of his way to help the other, and they had fun doing it. They went to movies together, to sporting events. The man would take the kid to his office, show him his business, take him out to eat, introduce him to his family and his church group. And all the time the kid was communicating a new kind of concept about the inner city, just by putting himself in a position to be known.

Meanwhile, our regular Young Life staff was growing too. We had finally been able to add women leaders to work with the girls—as was badly needed. I discovered that my own problems in relating with girls in my personal life was carrying over into my work as well. It took me a long time to accept the fact that I was goofing badly with one of the first girls who came to New York to work with us. I was unwilling to admit it, but every time this girl came into my presence I felt tense. She didn't like me, and I didn't like her. I knew I was responsible for supervising her work, yet it seemed to me that she took any suggestions as a personal insult. If the family of one of our girls was having a fight, and I called on her to step in and referee, she'd give me the feeling I was trying to play God by inserting myself into everybody's problems. She seemed to see me as a weak man trying to impose his leadership on the staff, and I saw her as a shrew who didn't know how to serve.

Eventually she bugged me into taking a new, hard look at myself and my responsibility as a leader. I didn't like the job of leading others, so I hadn't been giving very much of myself to this girl. It was much more to my liking to be out on the street with the guys. Developing the ability to be a leader of leaders was hard for me, and I fought it all the way.

One day I was sitting in the apartment thinking about this girl, and I began to realize that the very things that bugged me about her were the things that were wrong with me. God made me be honest with myself that day. There was no emotional crisis with crying or yelling; I just experienced intense embarrassment over how I had been treating her. It isn't very often that somebody blushes when no one else is around, but I felt my face growing very red. What had bugged me most was her insensitivity to my needs. Now, as I analyzed the situation, I could see that I hadn't been very sensitive to her needs either. It was a new view of the old formula, "Give love and you gain it." If you're always trying to bring love to yourself, you're going to kill it. I had been trying to get that through to the guys for a long time, but I hadn't realized I needed to learn the lesson myself.

It seems that all of us have certain qualities that are going to turn other people off, and these personality flaws get exposed along the way as you work and live together. Our natural reaction is to think, "Gee, I wish that person would change." But that person may never change. Our job is to change ourselves, not others. I can't believe that, with the help of Christ, it is impossible for us to get along with people. This doesn't mean we have to like them or what they do. We can even get mad at them. But when this resentment or bitterness hangs on, something has to happen. I don't think Christians have any right to hold resentment.

After that day my relations with this particular girl took a turn for the better. The whole experience taught me that I needed a greater sensitivity towards the needs of persons on our staff, particularly toward those who were coming into an inner city situation for the first time, for the cultural shock is tremendous, no matter how much they anticipate it and try to prepare ahead.

Our head girls' worker, Mary Miller, came to us from a small community in South Dakota. She had earned her Master's degree in social work, and figured she could anticipate the terrible things she would meet in the city. But suddenly she found herself undergoing the severest kind of cultural shock. Part of the problem she eventually solved by choosing to live in a middle-class apartment building outside the area in which we work. For her this was necessary and was successful.

The shocks do not all come in the nature of ugly, nasty things. Mary will not soon forget what happened to her on her first bus trip to Colorado with kids from the Lower East Side. A fellow was sitting next to her, and he and his brother had brought along all kinds of sandwiches and other goodies. She looked at the food and thought pityingly, "This is probably all those poor guys have to their name!"

A pretty smart penny-pincher, Mary was skipping meals on the way out so she could save her small amount of money for whatever proved important. She thought she could do without food for that length of time. But the fellow next to her said, "Mary, have you eaten today?"

"Yes, I have, thank you," Mary lied.

He knew better from the look in her eyes. "You haven't had lunch, have you? I've got a sandwich for you."

But Mary couldn't accept the sandwich, because she was embarrassed about taking from someone who had less than she had, so she continued to protest. Finally the fellow just looked at her, shook his head, and shoved the sandwich in her face. "Here! You eat this!"

Later that night when the bus was cold he brought his coat and put it around her shoulders. The puzzled way she looked at him made him say, "Mary, take this coat, and I hope that very soon you'll learn how to receive."

Mary has found, she says, a spontaneous acceptance of herself in the city. "It's a kind of innate gentleness, a protective attitude because I am so strange and new. It's beautiful. These are things I want to integrate into myself in order to become more of a person."

Like all staff members, Mary has found the myriad pressures of this kind of life almost more than she can bear at times. She was telling me one day, "I woke up this morning and I just couldn't stand facing the day." She had so many things pressing on her that she was overwhelmed. She hadn't stopped to figure out what all those "things" were, so she didn't want to tackle the work of the day at all. As she got out of her VW, a girl, one of the "10,000 things" weighing on her mind, was standing alone on the sidewalk waiting for her. And Mary realized, as she looked at this girl that she *could* separate herself from the abstract jumble of problems—the girl became a concrete situation that Mary could cope with.

The kids have this kind of confused feeling so often, and they haven't the energy, or maybe the discipline, to deal with the whole mess. So they give in to the helpless feeling and do nothing. They sit around and wallow in this misery, this sense of helplessness. They need direction and guidance, and here we can step in and help. Sometimes all we need to do is sit down and say, "Just pick out one thing and talk to me about it." They must have a starting point.

However, we can only help a guy when he wants to be helped. When we have to ask a fellow to leave we tell him, "Any time you want to come back and take your share of responsibility, you're welcome to come."

We try not to give up until we've tried everything we can think of. The path of least resistance is often not the path of love. I remember a time when two checks were stolen from a school, and no strong action was being taken by the youth workers involved. Dean Borgman felt so bad about it that he stepped into the situation even though he was not directly involved. By a remarkable bit of sleuthing on the part of the head teacher in the institution, and by one chance in a million for Dean, the theft was traced. Dean was cruising through a neighborhood where he ordinarily never goes when he saw two of our boys stick something into their pockets, then walk into a currency exchange. When he confronted them with the theft, they just shrugged their shoulders and said to Dean, "You don't understand our culture down here."

Dean took a very strong stand on the fact that they had robbed their brothers and sisters. They came back at him with the fact that he was an outsider, and didn't understand this kind of thing as a way of life. "We admit it's wrong, so everything should be all right. We'll pay back the stolen money, then let's forget about it," they argued.

Dean took a much firmer stand. He felt the theft should be made a public example in the school. Without calling any names, he really lambasted the kids who had misbehaved. He bared his soul, as he told them how he felt about punks who would do something like this. After it was all over, one student came to Dean and told him how much he appreciated Dean's being honest with them. But the significant thing he said was this: "You know, we really don't listen to you when you just talk to us. But when you get mad, then we turn you on and listen to what you have to say. Then we know you're our brother. When we see something really affects you and you've got the strength to say something, we know you're for us."

Dean and I talked about this later. What the guy was telling us was something like this: "All the blah-blah you give us in your common everyday moments gets turned off. We don't really listen. But in the dramatic, emotional situations—when you really get involved and suffer and take a stand—we turn you on. We hear what you say. You come through."

It's hard for leaders to accept the role of the blah-blah. It's hard to see how important it is to live in the blah-blah from day to day in order to earn the right to get mad when it's necessary. It's hard to have the strength and the guts and the control to step in, and to be able to do it without losing your cool. This needs to be done in an unsquare way which kids can respect, and in a way which gives them a chance to disagree. They may never agree fully with our viewpoint, but they can respect our becoming involved.

We need to remember that when kids call something "wrong" they are often saying something different from what we are saying. Perhaps, though, after each failure, their whole system of mores changes a bit, and through this kind of give-and-take a more helpful base of behavior becomes accepted by them. Perhaps it is best when we look for them to move, not to our position, but to a position that's as yet undefined. The new goals that begin to shape up for the inner city person are the result of this dramatic tension between us—they are neither their own old goals, nor our imported goals, but goals that are new and tailored to their needs. Our gift lies not in moving the ghetto person out of the city into the suburbs. It lies not in moving him from lower class to middle-class. It lies not in moving him from black to white. Our gift lies in our being here as catalysts, as technicians, as friends. *We are not here to put them on our agenda . . . but to become part of theirs.* And the full result is known only to God.

Some of the workers in any program have to be long-term people. We can afford a few people who come in for a summer, but I think we must always be careful to limit this. We need a solid, dependable thread of continuity in leadership. And the indigenous image must change from one of people who work for outside leaders to one of people who carry the load themselves, with outsiders perhaps coming in to work for them.

For years, on Young Life retreats, I was responsible for driving, speaking, breaking up fights, making announcements, planning skits, leading singing—the whole bit. It's amazing what you can do under pressure. You pray and you push and you don't have enough money, and there isn't quite enough transportation, and you can't make the number of beds come out even with the number of kids who are coming to sleep. Then all of a sudden everything falls into place, and you're not quite sure how. I can't imagine being in this work unless you have a sensitivity. You just "keep on keeping on." And sometimes you're not sure where your pushing leaves off and God begins.

Finally, after seven years, we set up a winter weekend in upper New York State, with kids from the streets of Pittsburgh, Philadelphia, Harlem, and the Lower East Side. I opened the first meeting late Friday night. After some humorous remarks I challenged the group to do something hard. "I hope we're a crowd that has the guts to listen seriously to the things we're going to consider this weekend." Ordinarily we spend this first night of a retreat breaking up fights.

Reid Carpenter had come with the gang from Pittsburgh to be the retreat speaker. He was a veteran with kids, but he was as uneasy as I about the four different city cliques all mixed up in one room. He spoke quietly, almost timidly, but he was right where the kids were. He called them "connoisseurs of wine," and some of them stood up to be recognized. Most, if not all, of them know what it is to stand around the project, or sit in the park, sipping wine with the gang.

Then Reid led logically into the New Testament. He led them from the story of the wedding feast to the Last Supper to show how Jesus Christ is the good wine of life. "Everything else we get hung up on is sour," Reid said simply. He talked about the way Jesus chose to walk straight through Samaria:

"God doesn't skirt the problems"; about how He sat down with the woman who had been an easy mark for the men in her town: "And for the first time in her life she could drop the things she'd been hung up on. She was free."

Everyone was tuned in now. "That's the effect of the good wine," Reid continued. "It's love. What that gal got was a little bit of God's love. And that was love like she'd never felt in all her life. Not sour stuff, but the best wine." He spoke so softly you had to lean forward on the edge of your chair to catch his words. The room was heavy with absolute attention.

The program moved smoothly throughout the weekend. Reid had set the pace. Bobo and his assistants, Frenchy and Tyrone, stepped into leadership positions for all the gatherings. I backed off to observe from a new perspective. They let me carry props during the skits, sweep out the recreation hall, assign sleeping space, and other incidental jobs. It was the first time in my seven years that there was enough talent for me to let other people take over! They did a beautiful job in every way. And it was the hardest thing in the world for me to step back and let them do it. . . .

13

Keeping Each Other Real

A FEW DAYS after Eddie came back to the city from College Prep Camp, he went away to school. He lived in Albany for two years, but during this time he would come back to the city quite often and talk to us about what was happening in college. In reality he was not going to college, but finishing high school, but for two years he tried to make everybody think he was something he wasn't because he hadn't yet accepted himself.

Accidentally, through contacts with Young Life-ers in the Albany area, Bobo and Clark discovered the truth. For several weeks after that Ed continued to come home and talk about his college experiences, but all the time we knew he was lying. At last Bobo and Clark and I decided to confront him. We told him how much he had hurt us by lying to us, and he became angry. Then tears came to his eyes, and to ours, and we wound up laughing and then praying together.

"It was beautiful," Eddie told us later. "Like a heavy burden was lifted from my shoulders. I felt free, I guess for the first time in life—really!"

We all need small group relationships in which we can develop this kind of honesty. This was the truth I had discovered back when Cross Carriers was founded, the fact that few of us can really make it on our own. We need to reinforce one another, to challenge one another. This is what we see so little of in our Christian society—so often there's the big leader out in front, minister and laymen are far apart, and the leader feels the loneliness the worst of all. The church needs to break out of its bigness and come back together in honest, vital, loving groups.

We need these group relationships to keep us really honest with ourselves and with each other.

The secular world is learning to cope with this same problem. There's quite a demand among the big corporations for the professional help of social psychologists in teaching employees to work as a team. The key is in helping top executives and all the rest of the personnel work together on common ground—to get to the place where they are able to be honest with each other, to voice their complaints and their compliments and work them out together. Each of us needs this kind of experience, for when you don't have a team to be on, nobody's going to challenge you, and you get away with murder all the time.

Perhaps the one thing that keeps people apart more than anything else is the fear that we won't be liked if people find out what we're really like. The Cross Carriers started out of a real need of my own; I told them I needed them with me, that I was down and couldn't make it without them. The greatest surprise I had was finding that none of this made me any the less the leader. I was still pulling them together, calling the marching orders. I was leading—but I was leading out of weakness. This was a very important lesson which few people seem to know unless they've been through it. You begin to see that you don't always have to be putting on a big show. People will respect you even more when they know what you're really like, provided you've been honest with them.

About the same time the kids were telling me to "get real," I started meeting with Tiff, the businessman from Wall Street. As the group evolved, I saw I had something special to learn. Adults made me feel insecure. I'd preface everything I said to them with an excuse. Finally one day one of the men said bluntly, "Bill, you teach us a lot."

As I mentioned earlier in reference to our committee, a group seems to go through the same developmental stages as a human being. The group is born when you first get together, and it has to grow through the baby stage where people talk on a superficial level. The only way I've ever seen groups get off that level is when people are willing to let crises take place. Some kind of explosion is needed to get the group into the adolescent period. This is where real honesty starts—some depth; some sharing of what you're really feeling inside; some doubting. If your group can never express doubt because the members are afraid of upsetting the apple cart, then maybe their Christianity is not a matter of personal belief but only of brainwashing!

Here is where a group can become a living, vital power. When you get a person who really believes, but is feeling guilty inside, the group can get him out of his shell. If he keeps it all inside, when he gets out into the world he becomes a phony, a hypocrite, a neurotic. Or he'll break completely away from his faith, and it will take a long time to bring him back to anything spiritual. A group can serve as the controlled laboratory situation in which a person can blow up and get rid of his load of emotion. If we really trust Christ, we will know that He is at work *through* the rebellion, *through* the crises.

We've been so conditioned by society to think that things fall apart when we're honest. We don't want a crisis. We don't want pain. We don't want suffering. But it's through these very things that the group grows up. It's not enough just to dump the garbage out, though; we have to sweep it up and burn it. This is where the healing power of the group comes in. The group, and especially the leader, must be strong enough to help the person find the antidote for his sickness. It may be in saying, "What are you going to do about that?" The group can call a member to a definite commitment, or at least to take a step in that direction.

You need a cooperative understanding when you commit yourselves to each other in a group—adolescents in a gang, or in a group, invite commitment. Teen-agers often commit each other to the wrong thing, but they *do* commit each other. They often feel a bond they may never feel the rest of their lives. This type of belonging should be captured by a group in order to promote real growth and life.

This love and understanding that allows you to take criticism, and give it, comes after you've reached the place where you can talk out your problems and get along and be real with each other. Then another explosion takes place to move your group into adulthood.

You can recite Scripture, read the Word and pray all the time, but if you stay in the adolescent stage of only reinforcing each other, you can die on the vine. You need to be sensitive to the crisis or explosion that will move you on into the adulthood of outreach. Somebody gets hurt or dies. A guy goes to jail. Something, however trivial, just goes wrong. Whatever it is, it serves the purpose of turning the concern of the group outside itself. A group alone is not enough.

At the adult stage a group's vision starts reaching out to the street, the neighborhood, the office, the church—all the various aspects of life. Here is the *strong* group—it's gone through the preliminary superficialities; it's gone through the suffering of being honest; it's learned how to take the storms, the ups and downs, the ebb and flow of relationship. It's jelling into a firm unit that can be knocked around, yet not fall apart. Now is the time to plan a definite strategy. Often I'll start by getting each person in the group concerned about being involved in the life of one other person. Maybe it's to introduce that person to Christ; maybe it's to help him through a specific problem; maybe it's to encourage him in school or on the job. Whatever it is, it should be a definite commitment to that one person. You reach out to him, and as you continue to do so, you come back to the group and share your successes and failures together.

Once the group has begun to taste success in this kind of outreach, it's time to start splitting off. You don't need to be in a big hurry to do this, but you do have to be sensitive—especially if you're the leader. During the baby stage the group will be very dependent on that leader. He directs, shows, explains, serves as a focal point when the group has no shape or strength or direction of its own. Then during the adolescent stage the leader becomes more of a peer—the group can rebel against him, or he can get the group riled up; it becomes more give and take. The group grows more aggressive, and the leader pulls back and lets the group take over. He has to be humble enough to stand back. A lot of groups die at this stage because of the leader's compulsion to be the hero, the charging knight. He must learn to listen, to shut up, to let the members start looking to each other rather than to him. This is, as I learned that night at the camp in New York State, a very humbling experience.

Healthy adults are independent, but "with the right sort of independence," as James put it in his first chapter. It doesn't mean that you throw over your relationships. Any time you encounter a group member after you've split off, you feel the bond. And you can pick up that closeness again so quickly!

Four groups have been especially vital to me in my work on the Lower East Side: one with the kids; one with our staff of leaders; one with the Committeemen; one with a group of local ministers. Each of these groups is completely different. I can't approach any two of them in the same way, but there are certain guide lines. We constantly try to get the group to a depth level, not by forcing or being phony, but by praying, by asking the hard questions, by making ourselves vulnerable, by being willing to take criticism, by being willing to be wrong, by not letting our own little hurts get in the way, by not being afraid to tell how we feel, by not being afraid to express love. And the love *must* be expressed both in genuine concern and in the asking of those hard questions.

You have to earn the right to ask hard questions, but once you've earned that right you're in trouble if you don't exercise it. Whenever you're afraid to tell anybody, no matter how strong they seem, you're headed for other kinds of problems.

Maurice Weir has helped me see this in my own handling of certain situations. Maurice is the youngest of eighteen children. He's married, has three children of his own, and is attending Queens College. Today he has developed into a fantastic street worker and has a burning ethnic desire to see his own people advanced. He sees it like this: "The whole black race is like a little boy. The whole white race is the big brother. The black man, tagging after the white man, becomes inferior just in the following. This shows he is not functioning properly for himself. The government, trying to legislate integration, is like the parent saying, 'You have to take Johnny with you.' The black, in a sense, is like a middle-aged man who has not been allowed to mature. The white man doesn't trust the Negro. He keeps running in to help again."

Maurice can tell me that he's glad I came to the Lower East Side, but he can also tell me that I have to step out at the right time. He sees Young Life as a valid instrument in developing black leadership, but he emphasizes to me, "You have to let us lead as we reach maturity." As Maurice and I got to know each other, he began to acknowledge me as a person, then he was able to begin giving himself. He began to trust me, and I became the first white he ever knew closely.

"You weren't just interested in converting me," he explained. "You would meet me on any front, on many different levels. I couldn't figure out what your angle was. You seemed to be genuinely interested in *all* of me. You didn't fragment me; you made me feel together."

I was no longer a leader to him. We had a two-way relationship. We were equal. Now as we share he'll tell me, "I think it's time for you to get a little tougher with so-and-so, Bill." I usually take his advice, and it pays off. Maurice's deep insight and wisdom have had a profound influence on the direction of the work on the Lower East Side. He has caused us to renew and rethink our strategy often.

From the beginning of man, people have joined together in groups. These have taken both bad forms and good forms. But people were made for each other. Man needs man. If we say we don't need groups, something in us needs examining! I know what it is to be a loner. I was with people much of my life, but I loved to stay clear of them too, because I didn't want them to know what I was like.

A group serves different purposes with different types of people. Some need the group for security. Their big goal is to learn how to feel secure within the group. Some need the group for survival purposes. The alcoholic, for example, had better stay in his group of AA; he needs the strength of the other members watching him and encouraging him. Then there are some people who need the group simply because they're strong enough not to need the group.

These people are secure. They're independent. They're healthy. They can go off and run their own lives, their own programs, just the way they want to run them, but sometimes they go off in the wrong directions. They need the group as a place where they can go for evaluation, where they can be honest about how they feel, where they can be free to accept criticism. God often speaks to us through people. The loner needs a place where he can listen to God through the medium of his committed friends.

A loner particularly has to develop the art of listening. It's so easy just to listen at the first level. We strip off the first layer of the onion, and then we don't want to smell anymore, we don't want our eyes to water anymore, we don't want to feel any more deeply. Therefore we condition ourselves to listening only superficially to what people have to say. What happens then? We miss what they are really trying to tell us. We come up with the wrong medicine, the wrong answer. We give answers to questions that aren't even being asked. This happens in the church, too; in any ministry. We're all set up to be a big leader, and we listen only part of the way. Maybe we're really involved with people, really understand the sociological structure of the situation and the dynamics that are taking place. Maybe we know how to communicate the message. But we don't know how to hit the core of life because we're only willing to go just so deep.

Unless somebody is challenging us to look at ourselves, to make us go deeper, we will always stop short of our potential. If I'm not free, then I can't free that other person. If someone is not getting depth in me, I'm not going to be getting depth in others. This is why even a loner needs a group. It's harder for that person who is not needy to accept the structure of a group, but he may be the one who will benefit most. I know.

14

Looking for Life

As Bobo decided to remain here in the city, to help his own community, other guys were heading out into the service and college. Clark had set a college goal for himself three years before he was able to get his credits all lined up. Then, all through the summer of 1966, it was a toss-up as to whether the draft board would get him before Westminster College. When it looked as if the service was going to win, he said, "Well, if that's God's will, I just got to be the best soldier in the world." He's that kind of man.

Eddie, who made the honor role at prep school, went out to Michigan to Hope College. He got into the habit of going to the chapel to think alone, because it was the quietest place on campus. One night he was sitting there reading when he realized Christ was saying to him, "Ed, I want your whole life. You've been jiving around for five years. If I'm ever going to do anything effective in your life, then you're going to have to go all the way with Me." Tears started rolling down Eddie's face as he realized that Christ's love for him was strong enough to be tough and stern. He told me later, "I'd just taken up His cross when I felt like taking it up—at my own convenience. And I put it down whenever I felt like it." Now he wanted to go all the way with Christ, and he figured it would take his whole lifetime.

Tap was accepted out on the west coast at Pasadena City College. His completely different environment there brings new problems into his life. "I depend on other people too much," he wrote back, "instead of on Christ. But I still think of that verse we learned in Cross Carriers, 'I can do all things through Christ who strengthens me.' He still gives me the strength to go on in my courses and with my friends and on the basketball court." Ollie, also a top basketball player, went off to Texas, and then got accepted at the University of Minnesota. Cisco and José had a rough time for a while, but they stuck it out at the University of Wisconsin. Maurice, a former high-school dropout, is a student at Queens College, where he is regarded as brilliant and graduate school material. At a session of the Joint Legislative Committee on Higher Education in New York, Maurice stole the show from college presidents and public officials as he asked the state to continue its support of the SEEK program which is sponsoring him and 1,400 other students from the inner city at the city university. The fall of 1967 saw twenty-nine of our Lower East Siders scattered all over the United States in pursuit of education, experience and a new style of living.

Meanwhile, big changes had been taking place in my own style of living too. Duke was the last guy I lived with before I moved out of 215. He had held me off and held me off, all the while jockeying for position with me. It was as if we were doing a square dance without ever touching. At first he completely avoided me, but he knew what I stood for. Once he became my roommate, I was able to find the spots where contact could be made. It was easy for me to be honest with Duke, and our relationship deepened rather rapidly. He was plugged up with bad feelings that should have been drained out years ago before the poison filled his system. Sometimes at three or four in the morning he would yell and cry and get a lot unloaded.

Over little things, like his wanting to get a car, we would almost come to blows. I had to show him the unreality of his desire, for he wasn't old enough to get a license. He got terribly upset while venting his suffering, but he would listen to what I had to say, and we would talk through a crisis and often pray about the resolution of the problem. These open-fire sessions brought us very close to each other and made us very aware of Christ.

We developed the kind of friendship that gave us a quiet confidence in each other. Duke could tell me how he felt about me, positive and negative, and I could tell him how I felt about him. He knew that if he went off the handle I would come right around the bend to have it out with him. We got a lot out of our friendship, because we were open and tough. Since he was attending Cross Carriers, and was very much involved in all our Young Life activities, I said to him one day, "Duke, I want you to go out to Colorado to be on the Young Life work crew for the month of July."

Duke had heard all about the ranches, but he had never gone any farther west than Ohio, so this idea appealed to him. Later I told him, "Duke, Colorado will make you or break you. But no matter what happens, when you get back I'm going to enroll you in Newark Prep." It was hard for him to believe that after his dropping out of school and leaving home, things were going to start coming his way for a change. He was particularly excited about the Christian fellowship he anticipated in Colorado. "I need it so desperately to survive, Bill, not only as a Christian, but as a person," he told me. He asked me to pray with him that God would break down his tough pride.

One evening, about two months before Duke was to leave for Colorado, he got so shook about a lot of things that he was positive even Christ couldn't help him. So he left his "C.A." (as we call our Christian attitude) on the table and went out to the nearest bar to get stoned. By the time he came home he was so drunk he could barely make it into the apartment. He stumbled around and woke me up, yelling, "Bill, I want to talk to you! I've got to talk to you!" At the time all I could say was, "Duke, go to sleep! We'll talk about it in the morning."

He told me later, "I could just see the look of disappointment on your face, and I was afraid you'd cancel my trip to Colorado. I began to see just how much you were really pulling for me, and I had let you down. I could feel something turning inside me."

Duke had already met a lot of the people at the ranch before, at weekend camps in the East. He had met the work crew boss, and as soon as he saw him Duke used his old talent of manipulation to get the job he wanted for the month. I had told him about the G-man job—garbage detail—and he thought this would be a great job for him.

Things worked out beautifully at first. Duke couldn't believe how open and friendly the people were at Star Ranch, and how easy it was to talk to anybody. But nobody's safe from temptation, even out there in the mountains. One fellow in particular rubbed Duke the wrong way. He was a big gang leader from Dallas who seemed to manage special attention wherever he was. George Sheffer, the camp director, knew he had a problem on his hands, and made a point of telling the guys from New York, "Just endure this fellow. I know it's going to be hard for you, but just try to endure him while he's here."

The way this cat ran around as if he owned the ranch particularly bothered Duke because he had been in a gang, too, only now he was behaving himself. Why should this gang leader behave so arrogantly and get so much attention? What Duke really wanted was some recognition from the guy. He wanted him to know, "I've been in a gang, and I know how to fight, and I'm tough, and if you mess around with me it'll be just too bad!"

On one occasion the two of them got into a little heated conversation, and discovered that they understood each other, liked each other, and respected each other. They wound up great friends. But temptation was still lurking around the corner looking for Duke. Cesar, one of Duke's best buddies from the Lower East Side, got into a fight with a young Mexican. After the fight was over, Duke suggested to Cesar, "Let's show these guys that we're really bigger than they are. Let's swallow our pride and suffer a little pain today." So no matter how much they felt they had been in the right, they went up to the top of the hill to apologize to the Mexican. Before they even got a chance to make amends, one of the bodies in the cabin rolled over and said, "We're not going to accept your apologies."

Duke's pride was really burned. He knew he could break that guy in half with just one backhand slap. As soon as he got Cesar alone he said, "Look, man, we gotta put our 'C.A.'s' on the table and beat these chumps. If we don't, there's something wrong with us!"

Just as they started over to fight with the Mexicans, Bobo and Eddie and Tap, who were all counselors, came out of nowhere and stepped right between them, announcing, "If anybody's gonna beat any butts, it's gonna be us!"

Here was a showdown. Duke literally had to suck in his pride and step back. But the thing that really crippled him was that these were his own buddies from New York standing between him and the fellows from a different gang. That just didn't follow gang ethics. On top of that revolting development, here was Bobo, a brother in Christ, leader of the Cross Carrier group, counselor at the ranch, defending the Mexicans instead of helping his own kind. "Why?" Duke screamed. "Why are you standing in my way?"

He turned and ran all the way across the grounds to Cheyenne Cabin where the group directors and counselors stayed. I was sitting there when Duke burst in and started screaming, "Look, Bill! To hell with you! To hell with God! To hell with Christ! And Young Life! And Star Ranch! All I want from you is a ticket back to New York!"

He was crying, and I waited till he wasn't making so much noise before I said as calmly as I could, "Duke, if you want to go to New York, just start walking, man."

I knew he couldn't go anywhere. He didn't even have a road map. But he did need time to get calmed down. I started asking what had happened, and as he was telling the story he got all riled up again. This ticked me off. I couldn't hide my feelings either. I wasn't going to pamper him, or pat him on the head and say, "You poor thing." I just pointed to the door and yelled, "Duke, get out! Just get out! Go! Find yourself a place somewhere and sit down and you talk to Christ. When you've cooled off, come back here and talk to me."

Duke went out and found that quiet place, and about three hours later he came back. We talked and we prayed. We'd been praying all summer for his pride to be broken, so I said to him, "Well, Duke, can't you take it?"

He thought he was pretty tough, but he couldn't take the idea of how he'd let Christ down. He felt he was a failure, and he asked like a little kid, "Bill, will this affect my going to prep school?"

"I don't care if you mess up from now until the time you go back to New York, you'll still go to school," I told him. "I didn't get you out here to bribe you that if you were good and worked real hard and said this and that, then I'd put you back in school, did I? Go out, man, and be yourself."

I was learning lessons, too, through Duke. Sometimes it was my own insecurity that demanded Duke make it, because I wanted to have him as a good example of what we were accomplishing in the inner city. He got on me once about that. I wanted him to speak at some meeting, and he was messing up so badly that he felt he couldn't talk about Christ. In my disappointment I told him he would have to speak anyway, which of course would have been phony.

Duke came back at me with, "What's wrong, Bill? Can't I fail any more?"

He was absolutely right, and I knew it. My own sinful self had been demanding recognition because I was embarrassed about admitting to that suburban church that my man had been messing up and couldn't talk that week.

Duke had really learned to ask the hard questions. "When I'm failing, you just don't like me, do you, Bill?"

He was hitting me where it hurt. I said, "Duke, I'm sorry. You hit it on the head—I haven't given you the freedom of failure."

I was worthless at staff meeting that night. I kept thinking, "Milliken, you've got to love people who fail. You've got to stay with them when they're messing up. You can't hit them when they're down."

So often we just don't let people fail. We've got to experience failure before we can really know how to succeed. If we could just know this and accept it and work at it! The whole Christian church needs to work at it. Our fear of failure is what makes us build up legalism.

That same summer I had to face up to something I'd been putting off for a long time. I'd been having trouble with my jaw going out of place, and I knew it should be taken care of. But one of my personality weaknesses is a tendency to just let things go. I'd been letting this particular matter go for a long time, until at last my jaw wouldn't let me forget it any longer. It couldn't have come at a worse time—just as orientation for summer staff began in June.

The pain in my jaw got so bad I couldn't sleep. This was a messy complication, since there's not enough sleep anyway during the summer. The doctor told me I needed an operation, but I said it was impossible at that time. I managed to talk him into waiting till summer was over, so he gave me some pills and told me to be careful. Now that's a ridiculous thing to tell anybody who's going into the summer months on the Lower East Side. Everybody was out of school and on the streets; I had the big trip to Colorado planned; I couldn't accomplish anything in the city or out west if my jaw was immobilized.

June and July, our roughest months, passed. I came back from Colorado. My jaw was getting so bad that in August the doctor forced me into surgery. To this day I don't know exactly what happened after the operation, but there sure were complications. The first thing I heard as I came to was, "Boy! This guy's in serious shape!"

As punchy as I was, I remember feeling scared. I opened my eyes and saw this machine next to me, and I had tubes in my nose and in my throat. A little further exploration revealed they'd taken out a tooth. I felt as sick as a dog, and started upchucking, and only then did I realize that my mouth was wired shut! They turned me over and blood was coming out, and they didn't know what was going on. They thought something must have ruptured in my stomach, so they rushed me down to X-ray and took pictures of me in just about every position imaginable. And all the time I was throwing up with my jaw wired shut, so miserable I just wanted to jump out the window and end it all.

Later I learned they had come within a couple of hours of doing an emergency operation to see what was wrong with my stomach. I'm glad they didn't, because two days later I was drinking liquid and it stayed down. In fact, I was out of the hospital in five days. The doctors concluded that the tube must have cut a small blood vessel which caused the bleeding. I had had that stomach ulcer several years before, so there was considerable concern for a few hours.

My buddies came to the hospital to see me and brought big jars of peanut butter—my favorite food—to tantalize me. I remember lying there, starting to feel sorry for myself. I felt so sick, and it was awful not being able to open my mouth, and I was hurting all over. I just lay there telling God off: "What are You up to, anyway?" I yelled and yelled at Him until finally I didn't have anything left to say. Then, when the bad feelings were all poured out and I wasn't able to sleep, I started listening. And it was beautiful! I just lay there listening to God.

Some of the thoughts He gave me were about patience and endurance. You don't understand suffering until you have entered into it. I was in a semi-ward, and the whole experience reminded me of how easy it is to live in a fairy-tale world, even on the streets of the Lower East Side. God was giving me the privilege of entering into just a little bit of suffering compared to the rest of the people around me, such as the man in the next bed who had lost his larynx to cancer.

God taught me some new lessons through this new stage of suffering. We need to be put in place every so often. Anybody who gets sick has a great chance to be awakened. We don't like it. We fight it, the way we fight honesty in a group. But it's the greatest thing that can happen to us. When we're flat on our backs, there's time and space for God to pluck out that thing that needs to be plucked out, or build in some new things that need to be built in.

I was only in the hospital for five days. But when I got out, I knew I had to go to Jeanie.

15

Missing Out on a Whole Bunch

IT HAD been two years since I had put Jean's ring in the safe deposit box back in Pittsburgh. We had only been engaged a few days when I had panicked and realized I wasn't ready to commit my whole lifetime to any woman. Since then she had dated several fellows, and I had built solid relationships with two Young Life staff girls.

The summer I was in the hospital, Jean was working with Young Life in Pittsburgh's inner city program, living in their first girls' apartment. One weekend while I was sick she came to New York with one of the staff men who was one of my best friends and who also was very fond of her. She was dating him at the time and had no intention of getting involved with me again. But I was never one to accept defeat. When she and I came together, the other people we liked so well faded right out of focus.

As soon as I got out of the hospital the following week I drove back to Pittsburgh to ask Jeanie to reconsider plans for our marriage. It was a rather strange thing because neither of us had expected it to happen, yet at that point we both seemed ready to commit ourselves to marriage. I guess all along we had never given up on the idea of marrying each other. After a couple of long talks, I went down to the bank, got the ring out of the vault, and watched her nose wrinkle up with pleasure as I slipped it on her finger. We both knew it was right this time.

Jeanie had already signed a contract to teach in Delaware, but she was able to cancel it and get on the substitute teaching schedule in her home town. During that fall she came to the city for one weekend. After a visit to the doctor, who promised I'd be out of my braces by November, we set the date for that month. Can you imagine being with the woman you love with your jaw wired shut?

I didn't see Jeanie again until the night of the rehearsal in the Hebron United Presbyterian Church where she had grown up and where we had met. My brother Bob officiated. A big delegation drove out from New York for the ceremony. I think they would have gotten there somehow if we had picked an altar in Cambodia! When Bob announced, "It gives me great pleasure to introduce you to Mr. and Mrs. William E. Milliken," a huge sign flipped down over the edge of the balcony where the Lower East Side guests were seated. As we walked down the aisle, Jean and I were caught between sophisticated embarrassment and outright laughter!

The sign read, "Can You Believe It?"

My main men from New York were in top form. And I couldn't mistake the gentle needle in their practical joke.

Long before the new apartment building had risen twenty-one floors above Montgomery Street, overlooking the docks, I had stood on the site and set a goal: "This is where I want to bring my wife some day." By the time I had persuaded Jeanie to take me "for better or for worse," the building was completed, and we took a lease on an apartment on the top floor overlooking the East River. On a clear day the Statue of Liberty reminds us that we are committed to the freedom that awaits every individual in our community through Jesus Christ.

Believe me, there's a great difference between living with a pretty girl, who is also a good manager, and living at 215 Madison! I rarely come back to 75 Montgomery Street without being thankful for Jean and for the home we share. Twenty-one floors up is only a low hurdle for most of the guys who want to talk, and Jeanie's presence in the apartment opens the door to the girls as well. The phone and the buzzer ring continually, and the elevator hauls an assortment of visitors up and down at all hours of the day and night. We're sure the neighbors often speculate on who it is that actually *lives* in Apartment 21B!

When the schedule gets so tight that Jeanie starts hurting for attention, I hurt too. At that point we have to block out a day to sleep late, to go out to dinner or see a movie, to go window shopping. Sometimes this means taking the phone off the hook or checking out of the neighborhood. But this is part of the new commitment. I would probably keep moving all the time if I could, and this temptation to stay on the go comes perhaps not so much from my feeling that I'm indispensable as from not knowing how to handle my own desire, or need, to give to others.

Jeanie introduces a new stability into my life. Her commitment to me is wondrous and unquestionable. She requires depth between us, and is not afraid to make me sweat something out if she thinks it will help us gain new ground together.

"I'm constantly trying to determine what is important to call to your attention, Bill," she explains half-seriously with an irresistible wrinkle of her nose, "and what is just satisfying to me!"

Jeanie definitely brings a new dimension to life. If I hadn't obeyed God, though, and come to the city, I don't think I would be capable of a marriage relationship yet. Leaving Pittsburgh and college had seemed like such a way-out thing to do, but because I could commit myself to God at that point, He continues to make life good.

Sometimes the kids come up to me and ask, "How do you give your love to somebody?" They live in a social structure that knows very little about commitment. When they hear someone say, "Give yourself to Christ," they may rebel because it seems impossible. They don't know how to trust anyone that much. Or they may have had the world pulled out from underneath them so severely that they're afraid to risk being torn apart again.

Gloria had told me when she first went out to the ranch, "I could definitely see I was missing out on a whole bunch, yet I couldn't trust." She didn't realize how lost she was until she got into an atmosphere where she had no alternative but to look into herself. Her home was filled with emptiness. The mother who had bent over backwards all her life to give Gloria everything she needed, had walked out to find her own happiness. Gloria was looking for someone she could care about, but she was scared.

"I thought during the week in Colorado I would take a risk; it wouldn't kill me," she explained. "But then I realized this isn't playing. This is for real. I'd be giving myself completely to Christ. And I didn't know what would happen. Still I didn't want to be alone any more. So I accepted Christ on this basis."

When she got back to the city she ran to me every time she needed to pray. She couldn't pray with anybody else. When I finally told her, "Look, Gloria, I'm not God," she was furious. She went home and got down on her knees, and for the first time she experienced being with Christ alone. She had no one to help her except Christ. "I have to trust You," she said, "and I don't even know You."

She did want to trust Him. It was as if she was saying, "God, You got to be more plain to me than You are. You can't be showing Yourself to me through Bill Milliken all the time." Through that one incident she began seeing God as One she could trust. It was a funny thing how she started seeing Him in her friends too, in the very ones who had made cracks at her and laughed at her when she first trusted Christ.

When Vickie first came and asked her for help in knowing more about Christ, it really shook Gloria. "*Vickie?*" she thought. "It can't be Vickie. If she has this Christ in her, anybody—*anybody* can get Him!"

This gave her a whole new sense of responsibility. "I can only tell her what I know," Gloria thought. "I can't tell her any lies." She wondered how she could explain to Vickie some of the things she couldn't even explain to herself. Such as the peace she had started to feel, peace that Vickie wanted. Gloria's problems had not ceased when she finally made up her mind to go to Christ. They had gotten rougher, but the Lord was giving her peace she couldn't understand. How could she give this to Vickie?

"I'll be dogged!" Gloria told me later. "Here was Vickie asking me to do the same thing I had asked you to do for me!" She had never thought she'd be in that position! This showed her how the whole business of trusting Christ could be a chain reaction. The two girls began to know each other in a way they hadn't dreamed possible. They had gone to school together and thought they'd known each other then, but they hadn't. This friendship grew to be entirely different from their relationships with all their other friends. The real Vickie and the real Gloria were seeing each other. It felt funny to be so open. They could easily have put each other's business in the street, but they didn't. They were making themselves vulnerable to being torn to shreds, but they dared to trust each other, and that made the difference. Christ was teaching them through little things, so little that they often debated with Him, "I know you're there, but couldn't this thing that just happened be only coincidence?"

Christ was hammering out His indigenous leaders, forging street rebels into responsible propagators of His love. "I don't want anybody looking up to me," Gloria said recently at a weekend camp where I had asked her to counsel. "I'm afraid somebody'll be looking up to me too much, and they may be watching when I do something wrong. When I'm just a nobody, life's easy. But when I have that title, 'counselor,' that brings recognition. The kids listen and they watch. It's costly to be a leader; I don't like it."

Gloria is still learning that if anything's going to be worthwhile, it has a cost. She still has to learn how to take failure, even to admit it to those who look up to her. It's hard for guys, too, to start taking responsibility. We fear being condemned. We fear being recognized. We fear goofing up a relationship. But once we accept the new position, we learn to be open to the Lord, and things happen. Even just in playing around or in other routine encounters with the kids, questions sometimes pop up, and we have to learn to say, "Oh, God, *You* answer. Please don't let it be me talking."

We spoon-feed responsibility in every way we can. Putting too much responsibility on a person all at once can break him. Here's where sensitivity is so important. You pull till it hurts; then you let up a little; then you pull some more. Responsibility, commitment, trust—the concepts so essential to leadership—are caught rather than taught. You have to allow people the right to fail, and then help them see *how* things went wrong and how they could happen differently next time. It's one thing to accept failure and mistakes as part of one's own leadership; but it's quite a different thing to give someone else the same kind of responsibility and let him be damaged by failure.

One of the greatest examples of trust is seen in the way Christ left His work in the hands of His disciples. He knew they would fall asleep and let Him down, but He knew too that He had to let them take over.

God gives us the freedom to fail. We are learning to stress this with kids who decide to give themselves to Christ. We have to tell them, "You're going to fall." Expecting failure is neither fearful nor skeptical; it's realistic. "Christ isn't going to leave you," we tell them, "but at times you are going to leave Him."

After seeing so many kids, I can almost predict what they'll be thinking a week after their conversion. First they wake up and say, "No, it didn't really happen." Next, they're going to make their first misstep. They're going to get mad, or hurt somebody, or go out and lay a girl, or get high—depending on their background. And right away they think, "Oh, man! I'm not a Christian after all!" We want to help them understand what they're going back into. We need to help them know the forgiveness of God—to know that when we fall down, Christ is here with His hand out to pick us up again. Our people in the city make such a fuss over the babies. Everybody in the park or the store gets a kick out of watching a little child take his first steps. And when he falls down or gets hurt they love to pick him up and wipe his tears away. No father's going to see his child fall down in the middle of the street and say, "You stupid kid! You fell!" and leave him there to be run over by a car.

Christ doesn't want us to get run over. He doesn't want us to die early in our faith because we stumble and fall. We have to learn to tell the new Christian how to put his hand up and say, "I'm sorry! Help me!" This is what forgiveness is; it's that simple. A look at life around us shows that relationships are restored by saying, "I'm sorry." The parent who doesn't teach his child how to apologize inflicts a spoiled punk on the world, and a lifetime handicap on the child. The realism of our faith requires that we let people know that they won't become perfect little angels when they commit themselves to Christ. They're going to make mistakes. But the great news is that they don't need to dwell on the guilt. The mistakes don't make us any less Christian.

What *is* a Christian? It's a Christ-one, a person in relationship with Christ. And when a person takes his vow to Christ, he becomes a Christ-one. After that, when he wakes up feeling great, he's a Christ-one—and when he wakes up feeling lousy, he's a Christ-one, too. It's the same as in marriage. I don't always wake up feeling married, or even feeling as if I particularly *want* to be married. I see the curlers on Jeanie's pillow next to me, and I remember I didn't clean out the car as Jeanie asked me to, and I think of all the other responsibilities of being a husband, and that kind of stuff doesn't exactly key me up about marriage. But it doesn't make me any less married. I took the vows, and became married. And deep down, despite the fact that some things about it bug me at times, I'm always very glad I did.

I think it's the same way with the faith. I'm no less a Christian when I've sinned. I've blown it, and I have to pay the price of blowing it. But when I asked Christ into my life, I took the vows, and I became a Christ-one.

So much of our expectation of others is based on what we expected of ourselves at that age. Our new staff people often need to work through this feeling that because the inner city kid doesn't perform on the same level they did, he's a failure. This is particularly difficult when we're working closely and sharing ourselves freely in the hope that our relationships can help to heal the gaps in all of us. When the kid fails, our own sense of failure is reinforced.

Really accepting the freedom to fail, accepting the fact that we are not personally threatened by his failure, enables us to be more objective about an individual, and more acceptant of him. And of course, this is exactly what we need, ourselves, when we fail—to have other persons accept us, support us, pick us up and demand or discipline when it's appropriate.

Standing by the Smith Project one night, Bobo and Eddie both told me, "We can't do it, so forget it. That white man's religion is no good." They were willing to say they felt prejudice, they hated white people. And their being able to say it was the turning point. They had met Christ, but they needed other little conversions. A person doesn't make it on just an initial conversion to Christ. The Christian life is made up of many little conversions along the way, and if we are not continually being forgiven, and turned back to Christ whenever we leave Him, we're in for real trouble. These little confrontations between you, and God who pursues you, come after the initial explosion where Christ comes in and you become a Christ-one. Maybe it's a firecracker. Maybe it's a cherry bomb. Maybe it's a rocket. Whatever form it comes in, the explosion breaks you open for other confrontations.

After Eddie had known the Lord a few years, he came to the place where he wanted to throw the whole faith thing out. This made me feel insecure and I thought, "I've got to get him back in the fold." The hardest thing for me to do was to let him fight it out alone with God. If Eddie really knew Christ, I was sure he would fight it out. If he didn't, then we were living under a phony profession, so we might as well chuck it and start over.

So often we panic. We say, "Oh, you've got to believe this," or, "You're going off the path theologically," or, "You can't do that." We get so concerned. This isn't trusting Christ to work in a life. My hardest decision was not to call Eddie. Then one night he called me from school. "I sat in the chapel tonight," he said, "and I started reading some sayings of Christ. I found I can't just play around, Bill. It's got to be all or nothing. There are so many nice smiley Christians around who are hurt and lonely and prejudiced on the inside. I had to commit my life totally to Christ."

This is another of those "little conversions"—the conversion to total commitment. We didn't realize it probably, but this conversion too was not final. People are always looking for that *complete* hookup with God. They're trying so hard to live constantly a pure, flowing, living, loving life. But the paradox is that if you try to have this constant heavenly hookup you never quite get it, because you're trying too hard. When you find you can't make it work, you become guilt-ridden and unhappy. You shut people off. You hurt them. You become critical of them. All in the name of Christ. When you're willing to say, "Christ, I can't do it. Help me get in the middle of life," you find Him there when you're not even consciously looking. And as you hook up with people you find you hear His voice coming through them to you!

Maybe yesterday you told someone about being free and alive in Christ, and today you can't even look at that person. Or you told someone to be polite, and then you didn't even hold the door for her. You make this beautiful plan about how life is supposed to be, and then you go and mess it all up. We make our nice little poetry of Christian love, and when we enter into it we find it's not so poetic because it's messed up by sin, and it can't be perfect until we're with Christ forever.

Society talks about "making it." People want the security to say, "Now, that's stable. That's black! That's white!" This is what happens when institutionalism sets in—"It's on the shelf. I've got it." People aren't meant to be this way. I'm afraid this is where death creeps in—when you put people into neat little categories: "There! I've got my little junkies. They made it. See my good little Christians." And when anyone stumbles and falls, the whole thing becomes phony; people start feeling guilty.

We need to free so many guilt-ridden Christians who know their Scripture, who at times really love and are compassionate, but who get so bogged down and so critical because they're afraid of making a misstep. Our need for security gets in our way so often. Maybe we need to take a look at sin. What is it? It's turning our back on God; it's refusing to look at God. This is the big concept. Once we've turned our backs on Him, we begin doing all those different things that we call "sins." Let's not minimize going to bed with somebody, or getting high, or stealing a TV, but let's bring them into perspective. When you yell at your mother, when you say something that will hurt a person's reputation; when you shut somebody out; when somebody needs your help and you walk right by them, or over them; when you try to outdo another Christian; when you raise your own stature by stepping on someone else; it's just as bad a sin. These are things that Christians need to remember.

We get so used to putting the "big old sins" at the top of the list, and making allowances for the "minor" infractions against love which are common to most of us. And we end up being clean and safe from the "bad" sins, but we go around hurting people all the time. It's using people for our own ends that's bad. What is love, anyway? Is it holding onto another person to satisfy our own need? Or is it being actively involved in the progress and welfare of that other person? And in all of this, all of us have to be willing to say, "Christ, I can't do it alone. I need Your help."

Although I'm certainly not putting myself in his category, I feel a lot like Paul at times: "There, but for the grace of God, go I." I don't think Paul was talking about how well he had it made. He just knew daily the constant struggle, and he understood the discipline it cost to be in condition for the daily rat race. But he was honest about his feelings: "I don't do what I want to do, and I do what I don't want to do" At one point he even broke up with his buddy and they went their separate ways. He was a very real man and he made real mistakes. He said in his letter to the Thessalonians, "Our behavior's been above-board"; we take that and mold it into, "Why, Paul must have been a perfect saint!" I think he was saying, "We're candid about our reasons for being here. It's not that we aren't going to mess up, or that we're perfect. You see us as we are. We're exposing ourselves to you."

So often we feel we have to proclaim the message, when we know we aren't close to living it. Maybe that means we're proclaiming the wrong message. The real message is that we believe Christ is the Answer—He is the one who makes life livable. That doesn't mean we won't fail, hurt, lie, fall down. It means He won't! In other words, we must proclaim both success and failure—how Christ produces the successes, and forgives the failures, sometimes even bringing good out of them.

Maybe next month I'll be as grouchy as can be, and won't even want to see you, but today I love you. And if I'm grouchy next month, God and you will have to deal with me at that particular time in His particular way. This is freedom—freedom to fail, freedom to rebel, freedom to back out, freedom to rise, freedom to go ahead. And we have to allow our kids this freedom. We can't reject them if they reject our kind of theology or our kind of social behavior. We have to allow them freedom to find themselves, and to find Christ—just as we did ourselves. If we're so insecure about our own faith, then we'd better preach something we're more secure in. I'm secure in my faith because I believe that whenever we have a free enough situation for God to be alive in, He'll be there, and we'll find Him!

16

Free to Go

God is consistently trying to get into our lives. His love is constantly at work. People shut Him off and block Him out and run away. But He is there, all the same. Knowing this somehow takes the tension out of us. We don't need to feel, "I have to bring Christ along. Come on, Christ, You're way over there; here's this person who needs You. I have to get you two together."

No, that's not the way it is. The deeper I got involved with people on the Lower East Side, the more I realized this truth. Before we ever knew the person we want to bring to Christ, He was already at work in that situation. Our job is in learning the art of performing the introduction! By this I mean breaking down the barriers, setting the stage, letting Him work through us. He called us to be reconciled to Him, and in turn we become reconcilers. I like that. I think the Christian fits right there in the middle. Where there is no communication, there is no point of contact. The Christian's role in society is to find the contact points.

A friend in New Jersey was telling me about his son coming home from a camping trip. He threw his pack down in the middle of the floor and just left it. The boy's mother, who had been cleaning all day, yelled at him for messing up the living room. Then Dad came in and added his voice. This was a bad mistake. Evidently the boy had been having one of those days in which he couldn't do anything right. He took refuge in his room, and his father went in and chewed him out. The boy sat there and listened until finally big tears rolled down his face and he shouted, "Nobody understands me! I'm lonely!"

Fortunately, this father was tuned in. He sat down with his

son and said, "Son, thank you for telling me. I'm sorry that we've had such an unrealistic relationship that you haven't been able to say this before. But do you also understand that your mother's lonely? And that I'm a very lonely man? And that everybody out on that street is lonely too?"

Then this man was able to relate to his son that what Christ does is to fill us with His love. This enables us to take our loneliness to the loneliness of others and find fulfillment. This is a beautiful thing. My friend and I began to talk together about how we think we give our children love just because we're together and we're nice to each other. But how often do we really give each other the thing that's needed most? The freedom to say, "I'm hurt!" "I'm lonely!" The freedom to express our doubts and fears. Why can't we give ourselves to each other in our homes?

"Give yourself"—we hear this term, but we don't understand it unless we're in the process of actually giving ourselves. We sit there watching TV with our son, or we read the newspaper while he plays records. We're giving him our presence. We're together, all right. But we aren't really giving our *selves* until we sit down with him and say, "Son, what do *you* think? I don't understand your generation. I know there's this gap between us. What do you think we can do about it?"

Making a person feel he is somebody, feel respected, is crucial in all the gaps of society. In the black-white problem. In the Indian-affluence problem. In the Catholic-Protestant problem. In the adolescent-adult problem. In the layman-minister problem. When we're always telling, and never asking, how can the other person feel worthwhile?

If we are interested in finding life, we must let Christ move us into the gaps where He will make us His agents of reconciliation. It's by entering into the gap that we are freed. It was through Christ's death that He was freed to be alive. He rose, and was born again. It's as we enter into these gaps, and die to self-centeredness, that we are freed to bring two people together, two situations together! I've never seen any other way of bringing together far-apart poles except to jump into the middle. We know we might get hurt by doing it; we might get trampled and knocked down; we might make a mistake. But this is what Christ has been saying all along—"Don't be afraid to fall. Don't be afraid to get trampled and knocked down. Don't be afraid to make a mistake. Because I'll pick you up. I'll wipe you off. I'll start you going again."

This stepping into the danger zone is just the opposite of how Christianity in general behaves today. Somewhere along the line we seem to have gotten the idea that the church is supposed to be safe and clean. We don't know much about forgiveness, yet forgiveness is probably one of the most important principles of the whole gospel. For example, when we deal with drug addicts in our community—and in some blocks down here 80 percent of the street kids are on drugs from the time they're sixteen—we have to be ready to practice forgiveness all the time. And we have to prepare our junkies for this same kind of action. In the first place, we have to face the fact that only a small proportion of junkies can ever be moved away from the streets and out of their sub-culture. Then, having recognized this, we have to set up a program that accepts falling, a long-term process in which an addict gradually learns to live with his problem in his home environment, accepting himself in an overpowering situation and gradually gaining strength to adjust within his familiar framework.

It comes as a surprise to many church people to learn that a guy can go back to his bag of heroin and still be a Christian. One of the letters Rick wrote me from the hospital, after he'd accepted Christ, screamed out his painful awareness that the Christian life is a battlefield. Actually, Rick's visible kind of addiction to heroin was little different from the various, less visible "addictions" Christians struggle with in nice, safe neighborhoods. The lust for possessions; the hunger for self-gratification socially, sexually, and even spiritually; the pride in being beautiful, rich, strong, successful, and a million other powers hang up neat Christians just as stubbornly as a needleful of heroin.

On the other hand, a junkie can solve his addiction by removing himself from the streets to the artificial climate of a hospital or jail. Protected from his real world, he can stay clean for years; but within a matter of minutes after he re-enters the city, he may run for the needle. Only after his insatiable thirst for gratification and identity has been satisfied *inside* can he come back to his sub-culture freed of his hang-up and capable of pointing other junkies to freedom.

What does this say to the safe, clean churchman or woman who doesn't know what it means to fall, to make a mistake, to get dirtied or bloodied in the secular struggle? Is his freedom from "sin" an indication of his holiness or of his isolation? It's so easy to be good when we're not ducking any cross-fire, when we're protected inside the circle of our Christian friendships.

If we're in the middle of a battlefield we're bound to have failures. But so what, if we're in the place where God wants us? Where is the church going to take its stand in those gaps in our society? Is it going to sit back around conference tables and talk about better methods without stepping into the conflict? If the church is going to concentrate on protecting its neat reputation, it's going to lose the reputation it hopes to gain. If the church remains uninvolved, it's going to die, because people turn in on themselves when they don't turn out to help others. No wonder people are rebelling against the church! It's lost its adventure. It's lost its charisma. And it's failing because it's afraid to fail.

We spend ourselves on big plans, on fund drives, on better building campaigns, and we fail to get down to the brass tacks of the gospel. The paradox is that too often Christians think they're proclaiming Christ, and they're really not doing it at all. They tell a story about this Man two thousand years ago, and they tell how wonderful Jesus is, but they don't prove anything by the way they live. They don't give their lives to other people. They don't put their lives on the line for somebody else.

What the church needs is for people to plop down their lives. Period. What's happening to the church is that it wants to take on all the characteristics of the disciples except the uncomfortable ones. It says, "Let's learn to love Christ more like the disciples loved Christ—you know, pray more together and have better quiet times." There isn't as much readiness to go out where we'll be blasted and criticized, and maybe get our necks chopped off. If the Christian's role in this world is to be an agent of reconciliation, then he has to go out where the people are—in the office, in the factory, in the house next door, in the street. And if he goes out he's going to get roughed up; he may even get soiled. But the church will be the place where he can come to confess his sin, to ask forgiveness, to cleanse his heart, to get ready for another six days of labor and of giving himself.

Paul told the Thessalonians how he came and lived with them and how his attitude toward them was one of tenderness, "rather like a devoted nurse among her babies," "as gentle as a mother taking care of her children." This is my favorite passage in the whole Bible. Nothing is as beautiful to me as this idea: We visit them in jail, give them the cup of cold water—whether they accept Christ or not. We're called to love, not to convert; it's God who does the converting. We're called to present the message as clearly, concisely, beautifully as possible, and to couple it with the tender love of a mother for her child. Where some divisions of the church tend to throw out the beautiful presentation of Christ as the answer to life's longing, others throw out the education, the housing, the visiting of the sick. The proper balance lies in the joining of the two.

We have to change our cities. We need to replace rotten buildings. We must bring education to the ghetto people. But if we aren't giving equal rights to their hearts, if we aren't giving them ourselves as well, the problem will never be solved. Nice, big, new houses don't answer the cry of the hurt heart. Any look at the statistics on the number of alcoholics behind expensive suburban doors will show that. Better clothes, better houses, better schools don't give the complete answer. People want more than material things, they want more than eight hours of your day, or a job, or analysis. They want your heart. But we have to give our hearts with no strings attached. We can't say, "I'll love you if you'll come my way, if you'll believe what I believe. If you follow Christ, then I'll love you." We have to remember He loved even those who did not love Him.

As we have found the freedom to educate, to house, to go to court—to give the cup of cold water in any form, here in New York—we've been earning the right to present Christ. When we live in the tension of the whole gospel, then we're freed to be ourselves to the people of the neighborhood. We're Christ's representatives whatever we're doing. That's the importance of living in the neighborhood. We're constantly exposed. When we're giving ourselves, then we've got the right to present Christ when the time is right.

The right time is often unpredictable, as it was with Shorty. I've loved Shorty. I've visited him in jail. I've had him hold a gun at my face, I've thrown him out of the apartment, I've helped him with the drug problem. And with all these things he refused Christ. Then all of a sudden, as I was walking down the street one night, Shorty came out of the darkness and we began to talk and finally he asked me, "Bill, what motivates your life?"

I looked at him eye to eye. "Do you really want me to tell you how I feel down here?"

"Yeah. I want the truth."

So right there on the sidewalk I was able to tell him about Christ. He listened and he wanted to know how to open his life to Christ. He may never do it. There are always the guys who never do. But my job is to give myself, over and over if necessary, and when I have the chance to present Christ, I do so. It's not as if I was coming in from the outside; I'm here as part of the community. My life is here, my heart is here, my soul is here. When I get the chance, I present Christ; when I get the chance, I give the cup of cold water—one is not dependent on the other. And along with the cup of cold water has to go the right for them to reject the message. Love, by its nature, is a choice. If we don't present it as a choice, then it isn't the gospel. Christ didn't say, "You *have* to be this way." He didn't run after the rich young ruler and say, "Wait a minute, you must not have understood. Let me put it to you this way." He didn't track down the nine lepers who walked off without so much as a thank you. He loved them and let them choose. And so must we.

At one of our men's breakfasts I talked with a neighborhood man in his late twenties. Everybody calls him by his last name, Stone. The only times I'd ever seen him before was in a gym—he's a great basketball player and the best handball player on the

Lower East Side. I shook hands with him and asked, "How are you, Stone?" And he started talking.

"You talk about this togetherness. This is nice, but people aren't really together when you need them. I wish it were true, but. . . ." Stone began pouring himself out to me. He'd just come out of a mental hospital after his second emotional breakdown. We talked for four hours straight. He told me, "I was bitter toward whites, and I took it out on them all the time. Then when I was down I went to my black brothers for help. And they let me down."

He became disillusioned with everybody. Nobody wanted to sacrifice and be hurt for his sake, and under the pressure he cracked. "I just went bazooey," he said. "I was ready to get a shotgun and kill myself."

I kept asking questions, asking, "Is this the way you felt?" And he'd say, "How did you know?" startled that I recognized the feelings. I pressed him into explaining: "It's a feeling that you really aren't there and that everything's so terrible and depressing. And nobody understands. I've tried to explain, and they just think I'm a nut. It's worse than when I was physically sick."

I told Stone about the time I had had to walk out on everybody and everything. I was very honest as I described my three weeks in Florida when I was trying to find myself. I told how I'd gone through those same feelings he had.

"Man!" Stone exclaimed. "We thought we were so different. I'm a lot different from you, and our backgrounds sure aren't the same. But we both got the same inside."

Before this, Stone had been so hostile; now here we were as one, sharing a common experience. That's what I call a miracle. "Let's thank God that we are the same inside and let's pray," I went on, "that the rest of this messed-up world can begin to realize how much alike we all are inside. No matter how differently we're conditioned, inside we have the same insecurities, the same breakdowns, the same lusts, the same pride, the same agony, the same joy."

This kind of oneness is what we miss when we build up that big shell around us. We have security in a sense, but it's a phony security. We shut ourselves off from real hurt; we protect ourselves so long that we no longer can be emotional and sensitive in the way we need to be to draw each other out. The subtle price we pay for that kind of security is that we can no longer be ourselves.

I was particularly moved by the movie, *The Pawnbroker*, the story of a guy who'd been hurt so badly by life that he couldn't come out of his shell any more. He shut off every person who came into his life, thinking that by not being involved in their lives he wouldn't hurt them. But the very fact of his refusal to be involved hurt them anyway. We can't escape this—if we shut people off, we destroy them, and we become dead inside ourselves. We have to ask Christ every day to rip out this part of us that holds us back, that shuts people off. Life was meant for us to be one, and it's when we open ourselves up that people come in and life becomes abundant.

Why do people respond so when they encounter a person who is really free to be himself? Because something greater than intellectual thought gets communicated, a freedom which allows the other person too to be himself. This is what Christ can do for us; what we are meant to do for others; what people are hungering and crying out for. But they don't know how to get it, so they run through a labyrinth looking for life, and in their very seeking for security, they lose.

This brings Christ's thought into perspective: "For whosoever will save his life shall lose it: but whosoever will lose his life for my sake, the same shall save it." We can see this all over the place in our society. People strive, and accumulate, and build a security wall to protect what they've got, and they lose life itself, because the wall gets so thick that nobody can get through. They go through life dead—very much alive in the world of things, but dead inside. They've paid the price of false security.

Our work here in the city expresses itself in different ways, in different moods. The apartment has one mood, the club another, the committee a third mood, the retreats yet a fourth. We have to be able to flow with the current up and down and all around. This is the key to survival—being able to flow with the need, with the times, being willing to change when change must come. It gets harder and harder to change as the mold starts to harden in an organization, but there's got to be an element of surprise in our work. We've got to be free enough not to protect ourselves against surprise.

Sometimes you don't like the surprise, but not being afraid to die is the key to life. It's part of the whole thought about avoiding pain. As Christ pointed out, if you're afraid to die, you'll never really live. It's the whole cycle of death and life—the concept of resurrection. I believe a work—and an individual—survives as long as you're willing to let things die and come to life again. It's when you try to hold onto life that it really dies!

17

Our Crisis—Yours and Mine

How can we begin to understand the suffering that a black man in America experiences today? How can we comprehend the ghetto, and the seething undertow among people who have been held down, until we enter personally into a relationship with someone who is hurting? You wonder why people blow up. Then when you begin to hurt with those who hurt, you start to understand. You see what loneliness can do, or rejection, or what it's like not to feel like a person. A growing number of American youth who are questioning the Establishment are swinging way out in their search for the answer. They may have a very deep meaning in the slogan, "Don't trust anyone over thirty unless he's been crucified." When you enter into a suffering situation your eyes are opened; you understand yourself in the light of the suffering of others. Your heart feels the pain of the city. You have learned to walk around in that other person's shoes! Only when this happens can you get angry enough to do something about the problems.

When you aren't in a suffering situation, you can't understand suffering because you constantly protect yourself from the hurts, the truths, the realities. Why does the average person get so embarrassed when a black man is strong enough to speak out? Why were people embarrassed when Malcolm X blew up? Maybe some of us feel that a lot of what he said was wrong, but we would also have to admit he said a lot that was true. I think this is why people were embarrassed. The guilt rose in them, and they didn't really understand it. A lot of our society is embarrassed today because people don't really understand. It's always the big incidents that are publicized. The hate forces are so often in control. Usually the other people are sitting back—quietly, piously, or fearfully.

The sickness of our society lies in our apathy, not in our anger. We sit back and let it have its control.

I had to learn a new concept of the city—much of the church talks about the city "where the bad people are, the delinquent, the skid row bum, the prostitute, the motorcycle gang, the dope addict. The city is where sin is." For many years we have seen the church retreat, until the average Protestant can almost equate his faith with blue skies, green lawns, two cars, and all the rest of the middle- or upper-class goals. It is interesting to note how the New Testament apostles concentrated their efforts in the throbbing cities of their day. Christianity took root and mushroomed, not in isolation, but in the cities. God so loved the *world* that He gave His Son.

When Christ came to the world of the prostitute or the addict of His day, He didn't hurt or embarrass them. He said, "You're forgiven. You need to be healed." It was to the religious leaders that He did His yelling, His preaching. I think if Christ would walk the streets near 215 Madison today, He would show love and compassion and care. He'd heal the junkies and the winos and the prostitutes. But I think He'd blast the grown-ups who scream at little six-year-old kids walking into a southern school. I think He'd blast the people who sit in church on Sunday morning and then go out to gossip about one of the members who has fallen. Where there's complacency and lack of involvement—this is where I believe Christ would come on strong today. I'd be very much surprised if He weren't walking the streets of the inner city and healing the "bad" people, and yelling out at the others who are all wrapped up in their newest neurosis, and unable to enter anybody else's suffering.

A new emphasis is being peddled around now. It's, "Look, we goofed!" The church is saying, "Go to the city now, because we've muffed it!"

We sure have muffed it! And the Christian world is going to have to pay a price for not being in the city. But let's not go as a bunch of guilt-ridden people trying to ease our consciences. Let's go because we have been given so much to share! It's like coming to the cross and being exposed as a sinner. We confess our sins to God and receive His forgiveness. We don't just sit there in our forgiveness—we can move out into life because we're free!

We have so much to give each other, but for those of us who are called to the city we must not go for the wrong reasons. We must go into the city because of the potential that lies in the ghetto, not because we feel sorry for the "poor people" there. We must get involved not because we owe it to these people, but because we love them as human beings. We must go because of the gold hidden in the mire, not because we owe something to society. We must go as aids and door openers not as those "in charge" or simply to give hand-outs! To be reconcilers—to be agents of healing—aiding our brothers in the pursuit of identity. We must go because we have much to share, not because we feel guilty about how much we have not shared. We must go because we need refining, not because we feel satisfied and superior.

The city is a great refiner. It exposes and sands down and grinds and shatters. But the results are beautiful if you have a community of love to heal you. Then, when all the elements of our society come together, that meeting, infused with the power of Christ, brings a reformation in all.

A society that is over-housed on one end and under-housed on the other is bound to wrestle with a guilty conscience. The prophetic voice of the city screams, "Hypocrite! Where is your Christianity?" And the church says to itself, "I know I'm supposed to love. I know I'm supposed to show compassion. I know I'm supposed to witness, but I don't know how to do it. I don't have an outlet!" So witnessing often ends up being another way of giving out knowledge without giving ourselves. We're not like the beggar giving that piece of bread to another beggar, because we aren't really beggars until we've entered into a beggar's suffering.

I hear the problem being expressed on every hand. Whether it's a Malcolm X or a stirred-up churchman who says it, I believe the problem is the same: the great lack of education in witnessing. How do we put our faith into relevant action? What *is* our responsibility in the church, as Christians, to the swelling, growing cities? What have we done? How have we failed? What can we do? How can we politically influence what happens in the city? How can we change a lot of structures that have been here way too long?

In our gray society I sense so much potential—a swelling underneath the surface. People who know the living Christ but don't know how to use their relationship. They say, "Christ is here. Christ is love. He is the answer." But they don't know how to demonstrate it. How do you make contact? If people are awakened to the grayness they are in, if the swell is ever united, great things are going to happen in our cities, in our suburbs, in our churches, in our lives! We must wake up and actually accept the fact that there is much more to our faith than verses to learn. Much more than a certain plan of witness. We must begin to act on the fact that witness is the total involvement of one person's life with another person's life, despite rejection, despite the other's not needing us or not wanting us.

We're conditioned in our gray society, even in our Christian context, to avoid any contact that might be embarrassing or uncomfortable. We don't like to enter into pain, so we avoid the race problem, the generation problem, the problem of loneliness, the problem of people being treated badly. Because—well, after all, people wouldn't understand. We hedge all around the key issue to play it safe. No wonder there is such a credibility gap. No wonder our younger generation wonders who it can believe. We must not hide the truth, we must say it as it is. We know THE TRUTH. We must let that truth set us all free!

If we really look at Christ's life, and not just at the verses we're learning, we'll be forcibly struck by His contact with people at the core of their existence. Isn't it impossible to understand the verses unless we're involved in the life? The verses mean a completely different thing when we're standing in the gap, making live contact. Christ didn't rationalize, or weave around, looking for the safe approach. Look at Him with Bartimaeus. It's obvious in that story that this man was looked down on—he was a beggar, a nobody, an embarrassing social problem. People might flip him a coin out of guilt, trying to make themselves feel better, but nobody was going to bother to make contact.

Christ could have avoided seeing Bartimaeus—especially at that particular time. He could have reasoned, "This isn't the place to talk with him. I have all these dignified people around me, and I want to be sure to preach to them, and not blow my witness for God!" But what did Christ do? He said, "Quiet." He walked right through the crowd, right through their nice little sophistications. This wasn't embarrassing to him. Here was a person crying for help, and Jesus was there to make contact with him. This kind of thing bothers contemporary Christians. If a teenager with extra long hair walks into a service—or an alcoholic, or a prostitute, or a poorly dressed visitor, or anybody who obviously needs help—what happens in *your* church?

The new man in Christ has to live in the tension of the social gospel and the proclaimed gospel. The new man in Christ is saying there is dignity in every human. We are to relate as persons, loving in the beauty of the differences between us.

One of the things I've learned is that when we see that people deserve this dignity, we can come out of our churches on Sunday morning strengthened to live in the tension with people during the week. In a church classroom situation we can develop the maturity of a group that is ready to look out into the community. We can get specific when we're together, and encourage and strengthen each other as we go out individually to be involved.

"OK, this week, who are you taking?"

"What can we hold you to?"

"Whom are you going to pray for?"

"All right, Mary, you're going to have lunch with that new secretary this week."

"Joe, you're going to get to that neighbor and really let him know how you feel. Finally do something together, instead of just talking about it."

"I'm taking this step with my kids."

Then we come back after the week and report what's happened. And when we come back, some of us will be crying. Some of us will be laughing. Some of us will be angry, frustrated, disappointed. But this is all part of it, and we help each other, and we learn together. When we come together we can actually see what Christ did through our involvements, or we can see how we bungled the assignment.

Christ says to us, "Come out in the boat, out where the waves are high. Leave your nets. Go out and be a person to others." Be vulnerable. Step out. Be hurt. Be tramped on. You're the one that's going to gain. Being a person to someone else is like a resurrection.

Only when you *do* it, does this make sense. Our shores are just covered with Christians who are willing to fish for guppies. They don't want to pay the price of going out into deep water. You can talk and even give sermons all your life and still not find life itself, because to feel it, to understand it, to know it, demands that you step out onto the fringe of existence. Out there you're insecure and insignificant, and the fog is thicker than ever. You step out—and suddenly there's life. It's you and God, and the fog's gone. You like it! You're free to go, and you're free to free somebody else. You've accepted yourself enough to go out and accept somebody else. You've become what the New Testament talks about—an agent of reconciliation.

It hurts before you step out. It hurt me when the kids called me phony or unreal. And I suffered inside and often felt we're not supposed to go through stuff like that. We need this experience of being crucified a little. And we wrestle with it, and we're ripped apart and we want to jump off a bridge and die. "It's harder than life itself," we cry out. We think we can't face it. Then when we step out we find it isn't harder than life—it *is* life!

We are living in days of great tragedy—days of fear, hate and anxiety. The boil of our society has been lanced and we don't like the sight of the open wound.

Yet there is Hope. The same Hope that came to us as a child two thousand years ago. The Hope that comes to reconcile us to the Father.

We must take that Hope and jump into the midst of the wound—to let Him use us as His healing ointment in the tragedy of the world. It will take a radical and tough love to heal our society's intense sickness. To do this we may have to ask Christ for a new set of eyes to see the things that we have been blinded to. To hear with a new set of ears. To let Him crush some of our old ideas, clichés and forms, to renew our minds from within. It may mean we will have to become less polite and step out from behind the skirts of the status quo. To get back to the frontier of life where Christ has called the church to be, down through the ages.